ARTHUR HAWES is an Archdeacon Emeritus of Lincoln and a Canon Emeritus of Lincoln Cathedral. He was educated at the City of Oxford High School for Boys, Chichester Theological College, the University of Birmingham, and the University of East Anglia.

Mental health has always featured in his ministry and it began in 1971 when he was founder chairman of the North Worcestershire Association for Mental Health, following postgraduate work at Birmingham University. From 2003 onwards he has been a member of the National Spirituality and Mental Health Forum. He was appointed a visiting Fellow of Staffordshire University 2009-2013 and was one of the two vice chairs of the British Association for the Study of Spirituality. He has published many occasional papers and contributed to a number of publications on Theology, Spirituality and Mental Health. In 2016, he was awarded the Langton Award for Service to the Community by the Archbishop of Canterbury.

HIGH DAYS
and
HOLY DAYS

VOICES OF THE CHRISTIAN WEST

ARTHUR HAWES

BALESTIER PRESS
LONDON · SINGAPORE

Balestier Press
71-75 Shelton Street, London WC2H 9JQ
www.balestier.com

High Days and Holy Days
Copyright © Arthur Hawes, 2019

First published by Balestier Press in 2019

A CIP catalogue record for this book
is available from the British Library.

ISBN 978 1 911221 65 4

Cover design by Klara Hawes

Contents

FOREWORD

Sermons are the means of expressing and exploring relationship, between God and His people, between the preacher and the congregation, between hearts that hope and selves that struggle. I was privileged to be a colleague of Arthur Hawes in the diocese of Lincoln. He is a person with a rare gift for relationship—through his own spirituality, his skills as a teacher and his deep love for people. These sermons invite readers to taste this gift and to be deepened in relationship with God, with others and with themselves. As the scripture exhorts us, we should read, mark, learn, and inwardly digest.

Alastair Redfern
Bishop of Derby

Introduction

This book contains fifty one sermons (and two long papers) used mostly on high days and holy days in the Christian calendar. I hope they will appeal to the many people who are housebound and cannot get to church but welcome an opportunity to read what is being said in the pulpit. I hope too that it will be welcomed by the tens of thousands of lay people who faithfully and doggedly sit, often on hard pews, listening to sermons week after week. They are to be counted among the blessed. Students, ordinands and perhaps some clergy might also enjoy this collection. We shall see.

The sermons are selected from ones I preached almost exclusively from the time I was Archdeacon of Lincoln (1995–2008) and subsequently. Why, it might be asked, did I always have a script? The reason is very practical. After preaching a sermon I would often be asked for a copy and, with no written text, I would have to return to my study in order to write one.

There are, however, other advantages to having a written script. Thoughts can be marshalled in advance so that they follow a logical pattern and the whole sermon revised so that points are clearly made and there is a balance and fluidity throughout the text. Secondly the danger of rambling is diminished and, interestingly, my wife always knows when I depart from the script because she says I start to ramble. Thirdly, if I am ever invited to preach again in the same church (which happens more often since I retired), a script enables me to check easily what I have said previously.

Increasingly church services are being timed carefully, especially in rural areas where the minister moves swiftly from one church to another and, having a script, means the sermon can be timed exactly. Time can then also be allocated for pastoral contact with people after the service which is vital to the ministry of any priest/pastor.

The discipline helped me greatly, especially in those churches where there is the tradition of printing sermons and sending them to a list of people, many of whom were not able to attend the service. A script in this case is de rigueur.

In this introduction it might also help to explain how I prepare for sermons. At the beginning of the week I check the readings in the lectionary for the following Sunday and decide which of them to choose for the sermon. I might then turn to commentaries for insights into the text which often include consulting the original Greek and only occasionally (because it is not a language I know well) Hebrew too, the value of which will be seen in some of the sermons in this book. I then make a conscious effort to let all this ferment for two or three days, rather like the leaven in the lump. At the same time I try to be open to the promptings of the Holy Spirit and the possibility of divine infusion.

This is a far cry from sitting down late on a Saturday night to prepare for the next day's sermon(s), a practice not to be encouraged, not least because it shuts out the Holy Spirit and does not allow for, what I call, fermentation. Situations have occurred which are far worse than 'the Saturday night syndrome'. There was a famous occasion in 1970 when I had been a priest for a only a few months. On this particular Sunday evening I was waiting in the procession behind the readers and the choir and in front of the vicar—my training incumbent. There was still a minute or two before the first hymn was announced and I turned and asked him what his text was for the sermon. He replied "You are preaching, not me". My anxiety levels rose rapidly and I said "But what am I going to say?" He replied "Tell them about God"— good advice—and so I did. Canon Derek Barrett now lives in Australia since retirement. Throughout my ministry, I have been very appreciative of all his support and help.

Now let me offer a word of explanation about the book cover. I am grateful to my designer son, Luke, whose idea it was to use one of my stoles for the cover design and to my daughter-in-law, Klara, for designing the cover. You will notice that it runs diagonally across the front and back of the cover. This is the way deacons wear their stoles. It is only after they are ordained priest that the position of the stole is changed so that it is worn around the neck. Deacons were appointed, we read in the Acts of the Apostles, to serve at table. They are then waiters and it follows that Archdeacons are simply head waiters! They wear their stole in a way similar to the way a waiter has a napkin over the shoulder. Not only does the stole provide a fitting design for the cover but it also carries its own meaning about being a servant.

Finally there are many people to thank for their support and encouragement and I would like to mention four by name. First there is Roh, my publisher, who has shown great faith in me, knowing that four years ago another publisher insisted that I did my own marketing which is not part of my DNA.

Secondly, I would like to thank the Bishop of Derby, Dr. Alastair Redfern, for kindly agreeing to write the preface to the book. Thirdly my thanks go to my family, especially Luke and Klara. I am indebted to Melanie, my wife, who has always been my best critic and read every one of the sermons in this book, as well as hearing them preached and reading the proofs. This, I reckon, is beyond the call of duty and I thank her for always being there and offering insights and comments which have enhanced the text.

Arthur Hawes
Shipdham 2019

The Promise of His Glory

In the Spanish town of Marbella—not the marina where the yachts are as big as houses—but in the old town, the church is dedicated to "Mary the Incarnation". Like so many medieval churches and abbeys, this one has many side chapels and each one represents a part of Mary's life. It extends from the annunciation to the glorification, from the moment when this young girl realised she was to have a child to the moment when she entered into divine glory. The birth of the son of God, Jesus Christ, ushers in the process of incarnation. At the heart of the Christian faith is a belief in incarnation, the truth that God lived and experienced the human condition on the very stage he created. The uniqueness of the Christian faith is not to be found in a belief in one God or in the hope of eternity or in a code for living based on the scriptures, but in God becoming human. It was Irenaeus who said that God became human, so that human beings could become divine. Incarnation is the one unique difference between the Christian faith and the eight other major religions in the U.K.

The baptism of Jesus celebrated early in the new year adds to our understanding of the meaning of incarnation. John was not even sure if he should be baptising Jesus. If he truly was the Messiah—God's anointed one—then surely he did not need to be baptised. Now, Jesus' answer is interesting.

"Let it be so now; for it is proper for us in this way to fulfil all righteousness."

Jesus makes it very clear to John that he does need to be baptised in order to "fulfil all righteousness". I understand these words to mean that Jesus is a human being like you and me and it is part of God's intention to share our humanity and therefore to be confined in time and space as we are and to undergo the same initiation ceremonies that we do. In the Christian faith initiation is by baptism and so Jesus needs to be baptised like anyone else. This sets a pattern for the future because what it means is that the Son of God is not to be allowed to escape any human experience simply because he is the Son of God. The Gospels themselves are testimony to this truth and we find the Jesus of the Gospels expressing emotion. We read about him being angry, sad, reduced to tears, with a wry smile on his face, and filled with joy when he takes young children into his arms. Incarnation, then, means God entering fully into the human enterprise in the person of Jesus. Jesus is to be spared nothing and, of course, there is no greater example of this than his excruciating pain on a cross.

I was the co. chairman of the National Spirituality and Mental Health Forum. My co. chairman was from the Janki organisation and treasurer from the Muslim faith. It began as a result of 9/11 when there were and continue to be fears for Muslims living in the west and most particularly for their mental health. The single most important lesson that I have learnt since the Forum began is that people from the other world faiths know what they believe. What they ask of Christians is that they state unequivocally what they believe. Unpacking the uniqueness of the incarnation—the Christmas message gives us a beginning. Here we can resonate with Mary and share her political agenda articulated in the words of her song, the Magnificat. Incarnation means identifying with the downtrodden, the poor, the marginalised, those whose inner lives are blighted by mental health problems, those assailed by a range of disabilities, and those who live their lives on the edge of society. In all our large cities at Christmas time there are thousands of volunteers working with charities like Crisis which seeks to support many of those I have just identified. When we recall that the saviour of this world was given a feeding trough for a cradle, died on a cross where the city tipped its rubbish and was buried in a borrowed grave, incarnation is about getting our hands dirty and entering fully into the human condition—its pain and bleakness, its tragedy and sin, as well as its joy and celebration and its hope and glory.

As the name of the National Forum implies, the word on the street that brings all of this together is the one word "spirituality". Now is the time for the Christian church to identify and proclaim its own unique spirituality. I suggest this begins with understanding the great truth that God became man, and as John Betjeman writes,

No love that in a family dwells,
No caroling in frosty air,
Nor all the steeple-shaking bells
Can with this single Truth compare –
That God was Man in Palestine
And lives to-day in bread and wine.

It is worth reminding ourselves that the celebration of Christmas, the celebration of incarnation, the celebration of Emmanuel—God with us—extends from Advent Sunday to Candlemas on February 2nd. This means it includes the four weeks of preparation before Christmas, the Christmas festivities and of course the celebration of the Epiphany. Today we are thinking about Jesus' incarnation and then finally the season known as the "Promise of his glory" ends with Candlemas when Jesus is presented as a young child in the temple. It is here that he meets the old Simeon and Anna. St Luke attributes to Simeon the words of the Nunc Dimittis in which he proclaims that Jesus is a light to the gentiles and the glory of the people of Israel.

I am told that the Christmas tree in Buckingham Palace will come down before the Epiphany. This is understandable as the Queen is in North Norfolk and will be for the next 2 months. I hope that you have not yet dispensed with all your Christmas decorations and that you will continue to celebrate the incarnation—the Feast of God with us—until the 2nd February. It is only then that we can turn our eyes to that other great Christian festival, Easter with its promise of resurrection and hope for the future. Meanwhile as people who carry the name of Christ, as Christians, let us get on with God's work in the world and truly become his hands, his feet, his eyes and his voice. It is a wonderful ministry which we are all invited to share and my hope and my prayer is that everyone will do just that, Amen.

Prayer

O God who fulfils your promises for the whole of humanity, recreate in us the truths of the great festivals of Christmas, the Epiphany and the Presentation. May the promise of your glory become a reality for all people, Amen.

Mind the Gap

Sixteen years of my ministry was spent near what the city signs describe as the fine City of Norwich. Among my responsibilities was being the incumbent of three small Norfolk villages lying about eight miles north of Norwich. The Christmas and Epiphany services were shared between the three of them and each had its own crib. Interestingly, the three cribs were very different. In one, it was no more than a shelter over a feeding trough—a simple structure to keep the food dry. In another, it was more like a traditional stable—an enclosed building to keep both the food and animals dry and warm. The third, on the other hand, was designed like a house with doors, windows—a very well-appointed haven for animals.

The second crib, most like a stable, would have been the one usually associated with the stable in Bethlehem. It is the type of crib that features in nativities across the country; crowding into the scene is not only the Holy Family, but shepherds, wise men, animals and angels.

You know only too well that an ever-widening gap has been developing between the Church and the world in our society. As we are so often reminded when we travel on the underground—mind the gap! Christmas and indeed Epiphany are no exception. This gap, or what many refer to as "disconnectedness", is well illustrated by what we hear in shops, particularly those selling greetings cards. One person was heard to say on picking up a Christmas card of the Nativity scene, "Now they are bringing religion into Christmas". On another occasion, a shopper asked for a baptism card and was told by the assistant that they were in the religious section and were put away over Christmas.

This gap, this disconnectedness, is the more pertinent when we recall that Jesus died for the world, not for the church. Our faith, the Christian faith, is incarnational. It is about God identifying with the created order, about becoming a human being, about Christmas, about closing the gap, and about being connected. Our faith is about real people living in the real world, which is why we love to identify with the Christmas scene. Here was a baby, the stuff of human life, a family, visitors from near and far. Given that the shepherds were Jewish and the Wise Men Gentiles, the Jewish understanding was that the whole world had come to visit the child. Epiphany articulates the universality of Christ. Who are these Magi? No less a person than the Archbishop of Canterbury has his doubts. It is unclear how many of them there were. According to tradition there were three Wise Men because three presents were offered to the young child. Magi were people who searched the outer realms and spaces, but like all of us, they too had an inner life. One of the first things human beings learn is to separate and disconnect the inner life from the outer life. The question for us—the great spiritual question—is how we reconnect God with ourselves, how we reconnect our inner life with our outer life and close the gap. We learn about reconnecting from our visit to the child in Bethlehem. One modern carol describes the Christ child like this:

"Star child, earth child,
Hope-for-peace child,
God's stupendous Son".

Clues about closing the gap abound in the days that follow Christmas, packed with festivals and celebration. In our modern liturgy we celebrate the "Promise of his Glory" from the beginning of Advent until Candlemas. There are clues in the presents which the visitors brought. They represented money, mystery and mortality. The first present was gold, which traditionally is given to a king, and kingship was identified in this young child. Gold is a precious metal and for centuries has been standard currency representing a nation's wealth and continues to be valued as such today. Gold coins have been replaced by copper and paper money and, they in turn, by the credit card. It is all too easy for our financial transactions to become impersonal and lack any sense of value. Yet, it seems to me, when we give money for a particular cause or charity, we are in fact giving part of ourselves and so the gift can be a personal donation and an individual offering. So it was that the visitor who gave gold to the young child also gave a part of himself. The inner and outer are connected.

The second gift was frankincense, which was used in Jewish worship. The smoke from the incense became associated with prayers rising heavenwards. I think its origins may well have been of a more practical nature because, when animal sacrifices were being prepared, the sweet smell of incense helped to counteract the smells from the altar. What the smoke from the incense can do in worship is heighten our awareness of the numinous and so help produce a sense of mystery and holiness. In any understanding of God we need to hold on to a sense of mystery because God is not wholly explicable, totally understandable in human terms or able to be fully expressed in human symbol and language. Part of God is beyond us and beyond our comprehension and beyond the outer realms and spaces. Part of the very definition of God is that he is greater than the creation and beyond human understanding and reasoning. That is not to say that we cannot approach God and meet him face to face. This is the truth that lies at the heart of Christmas and Epiphany because here, in the child Jesus, we believe we see God. However, there is a sense of otherness and mystery, which the second gift from the Three Kings identified.

The third present was myrrh, which was the ointment used in the preparation of bodies, not dissimilar from some of the preparations used in embalming. This gift directed attention to Jesus' death, though it is unclear whether the donor had any awareness or insight of the premature death which lay ahead of this young child. What the gift does is point to a truth about humanity, which is that human beings are born, live their lives and then die. The truth is that to be human means to be mortal, to be finite, to have beginnings and ends and Jesus expresses this truth in his own human existence. Acknowledgement of our own mortality helps us to avoid the temptation of equating ourselves with God—a temptation all too common in our culture, not least in the world of finance.

There are innumerable ways of communicating. Today we rely heavily upon the mobile phone and the email. In the world of Harry Potter, the reliance was upon owls. In the early stories of the Gospels the chosen means of communication is through dreams and angels. The Magi were warned in a dream not to return to Herod, but to go home another way. What would be quite wonderful is, if all of us who have journeyed to see the Christ child with the Wise Men this Christmas, were able to return another way. That is to say, that through the very experience of living and worshipping at the festivals of Christmas and Epiphany once again, we are changed in such a way that our lives take a different route and one which will take us nearer to the heart of God, more aware of his otherness, continuing presence, mystery and abiding love.

Prayer

We pray that all the events of Christmas and the Epiphany will encourage and enable us to ensure that the faith of Christ is rooted in the world. Just as Jesus was one with God the Father, so we pray that the church will reflect that oneness and unity in the world today, Amen.

Candlemas

He was an old and devout man sitting on a seat perhaps talking to other old men and doing what old people do. Really old people sit a lot, like to talk about the past (what in Norfolk is known as mardling), say how much better things used to be, often are amazed at some of the new inventions and the things young people get up to, and then through rheumy eyes observe what is going on around them. Old people are very good at observing and often have a skill which comes from age, of being able to sum up in quite a crisp way what they have been observing and the context in which the observations were made. This particular old man was called Simeon and it would appear that he was a devout Jew who said his prayers regularly and observed the festivals of the church. Little did he know that he was going to provide a Feast Day for the Christian church.

What old Simeon observed was a baby boy and his parents and, I imagine, he might have looked very closely at the faces of the parents and the face of the young child. Before him there had been shepherds and wise men all of whom had come to look at this child and even to bring gifts. Now it was old Simeon's turn and he saw what they saw. He saw looking up at him in the face of this young child the face of God. When he spoke, he spoke the words of what today we call the Nunc Dimittis. He said that his eyes had seen the salvation which God had prepared for everyone to see. This is what he observed and he went on to say more about the future of the young child.

The day that has been set aside to celebrate Jesus' arrival at the temple is called Candlemas or the Feast of the Purification or the Presentation of Christ in the Temple. It is also known as the Feast of Light for the World and in the Orthodox church the Feast of Meeting. The Orthodox celebrate the meeting of Simeon with Mary, Joseph and the baby and, at the same time, they celebrate the meeting of people with the presence of God. The several names by which this feast has been known in Christian history illustrate just how much there is for us to learn about it. Perhaps the strongest attraction of Candlemas is the 'bitter-sweet' nature of what it celebrates. It is a feast day and the arrival of the child, Jesus, in the temple, greeted first by Simeon and then by Anna, calls for rejoicing. Nevertheless, the prophetic words of Simeon, which speak of the falling and rising of many and the sword that will pierce, lead on to Holy Week and Easter. The scriptures and the services of the Christmas season have several pointers to the suffering of the Jesus, but none more potent than the words of Simeon—coming as they do at the very end of the Christmas season and with Lent nearly always very close, they make Candlemas a pivot in the Christian year. Our celebration of the presence of God and the light of Christ is then a very important occasion.

I have four 'Cs'. Candlemas is my first 'C'. My second 'C' stands for catechumen. Catechumens are christians in training. One book says this:

"The systematic instruction and formation of its catechumens is a solemn responsibility of the Christian community." Traditionally, the preparation of catechumens is a responsibility of the Bishop, which is shared with the priest, deacons, and appointed lay catechists of the diocese. The sponsors are called catechists who generously have agreed to support the candidates. There is much to learn, but central to the training is an opportunity to discover more about the presence of God and the way in which God makes himself known to people.It is an opportunity for 'meeting' which is one of the meanings of Candlemas. Just as Jesus was called the 'Light of the World' so Christians are to be 'lights' shining in the darkness. Today it is not easy for young people to be Christians, indeed it is not easy for anybody to be a Christian and this is because we live in an age where the church, even though in the Diocese of Lincoln there are 659 church buildings, has been marginalized and often people are critical of the church and what it stands for. Sometimes they are even hostile. I know of a church in the city of Lincoln which regularly has all its windows broken and it costs a lot of money for the congregation there to keep replacing them.

My third 'C' is for commission. Catechumens are commissioned before they begin their course of training; after which they are ready to be presented to the Bishop who will then confirm them.

Confirmation is the fourth 'C' and it means that not only will the candidates be confirmed in their faith publicly and make a public declaration of their belief, but the meaning of the word itself is one which suggests that they will be given the strength and the grace of God. The period of training and preparation culminates in confirmation which is a sacrament. A sacrament is 'an outward and visible sign of an inward and spiritual grace'. The task following confirmation is to make clear and plain the presence of God in the daily lives of ordinary people. This is what we have to learn and this is the challenge that lies ahead of all of us. For me it is a privilege to be here at this service tonight at the beginning of an important innovation. Not only is the training of catechumens a new venture for the parish but I believe a new venture in the Diocese. It is a new way of doing things and a practice which I hope will be used and copied in many other parishes. Certainly, with your vicar's permission, I want to take a copy of tonight's service to the Bishop and his staff for them to see. We all have gathered to celebrate Candlemas, to commission catechumens in preparation for their confirmation. Please remember these four words beginning with 'C':

Candlemas
Catechumen
Commission
Confirmation

and when you are old, like Simeon, I hope you will be sitting down and reminiscing with other old people and remembering this night when you became a catechumen and were commissioned in preparation for confirmation. In years to come I hope you will also remember ways in which you became aware of the presence of God in your life and how you helped other people to see God in their lives. Think of old Simeon, he is an important person in the bible and one whom I am sure will have a very special place in your hearts and devotions.

Prayer

Almighty Father whose Son Jesus Christ was presented in the Temple and acclaimed the glory of Israel and the light of the nations: grant that in him we may be presented to you and in the world may reflect his glory. Be with all those who are preparing to take their full part in the life of the Christian community. All this we ask in the name of Jesus Christ our Lord, Amen.

Counter Cultural

The sermon on the Mount in St Matthew's gospel is the largest tract of teaching in the four gospels. Jesus as usual turns everything on its head and upside down; for example—love your enemies.

The Christian faith, as we know, is full of paradox, something with which the Church of God has always had to contend— quite simply that the Gospel of Jesus, like Jesus himself, is often counter-cultural; that is to say that the truths of the Gospel— truth about God, truth about Jesus, truth about being human, and truth about you and me—do not sit comfortably with our society and the world we inhabit.

It is not easy being a Christian today (perhaps it never has been) and it can be very difficult to preach the Gospel and know how to engage with our world, its young people and its young families. What then is happening to bring about this separation of God from the world and increasing privatisation of the Church so that it becomes a club for the converted and initiated. Let me identify six phenomena. Once we have named them, perhaps we shall be better equipped to meet the challenges of 21st century living.

First there is amorality, not immorality. Amorality means no morality, the absence of a moral code. So much of what we do and say is understood and explained in terms of human behaviour, our genetic blueprint, the environment which formed us, what we learned from our parents, and how we have interpreted for ourselves the world around us. If a person has no sense of right or wrong, no moral code, then it is difficult, perhaps impossible, to be able to choose between right and wrong. It really does make sinning very difficult!

Some have described relativism as the curse of our age. What this means quite simply is that we no longer have available to us universal and absolute truths which have stood the test of time. Thinking has been replaced by feeling. It is what you feel that justifies what you do and how you do it. The age of rationalism is past. Now everything is relative to the society in which we live, to the community to which we belong and the culture around us. This relativism is linked to the third phenomenon and that is individualism. Individualism is not the same as individuality. Jesus had a lot to say about and to individuals. He honoured and respected individuals but, at the same time, saw them as belonging to families and communities. Individualism gives rise to phrases like 'what matters is what matters to me'. This stress on individualism does nothing to promote the family or the local community. Rather it results in a lot of people becoming isolated and lonely. Did you know, for example, that 40% of all households in the U.K. have only one person living in them?

All of this can be very confusing and disturbing. It is not helped by two further factors. When people feel worried and concerned, they look for something reliable that will provide them with certainty. What this does, in turn, is fuel fundamentalism— another issue. We need only to look around the world to see the fruits of fundamentalism, most especially in the Middle East. What is provided is a false security—something which is not grounded in faith and love. God may have become separated from the world in people's minds but there is still a craving for the spiritual life—for something which is beyond what we can see and touch. We know too that, where there is a vacuum, other things will move in to fill the space.

Yet another phenomenon of our age is superstition. Think, for a moment if you will, about the numbers of Mystic Megs and clairvoyances, the increasing sales of Tarot Cards and ouija boards. Did you know that in France there are now more fortune tellers than there are clergy. All of this adds up to superstition and there is no place for superstition in the Christian faith.

Finally we need to recognise that we live in a very visual world. Communication is through the television, the computer, the iphone (9 or even X)—so much information is made available in visual form. How then do we communicate something like mystery, holiness, the love of God, the redeeming power of Jesus, the presence of the Holy Spirit, eternity, the otherness of God— what pictures do we use to express these riches of our Christian faith? We must find visual means of communication because we live in an age where seeing really *is* believing.

It can be a very confusing world and a world where it is not easy to be a Christian. So, hold fast to your faith, be firmly rooted in the love of God, be confident in communicating the Gospel, be imaginative in the way that you talk about the things of God, and never stop being courageous and full of hope that the glory of God will shine in the dark places of the earth.

Something which is visible and tangible and which I believe is an asset are our church buildings. We must not be afraid to continue to utilize our buildings for the Mission of the Church. So let me finish with some words written about church buildings …. 'We in England live in the chill religious vapours of Northern Europe, where moribund religious establishments loom over populations that mostly do not enter churches for active worship even if they entertain inchoate beliefs. Yet these establishments guard and maintain thousands of houses of God, which are markers of space and time. Not only are they markers and anchors, but also the only repositories of all-embracing meanings and point beyond the immediate to the ultimate. They are the only institutions that deal in tears and concern themselves with the breaking points of human existence. They provide frames and narratives and signs to live by, and offer persistent points of reference. They are repositories of signs about miraculous birth and redemptive sacrifice, shared tables and gift-giving; and they offer moral codes and exemplars for the creation of communal solidarity and the nourishment of virtue. They are places from which to launch initiatives which help sustain the kind of networks found, for example, in the inner city, they welcome schools and regiments and rotary clubs; they celebrate and commemorate; they are islands of quietness; they are places in which unique gestures occur of blessing, distribution and obeisance; they offer spaces in which solemnly to gather, to sing, to lay flowers, and light candles. They are—in Philip Larkin's phrase—serious places on serious earth. (Martin 1991:1).

[I am indebted to Bishop David Connor for many of the ideas developed in this sermon]

Prayer

We ask your help, good Lord, to understand the age in which we live and for us to be able to communicate and make visible the truths of the gospel and the values of spirituality in today's world. We pray that we may be in the world, but not of the world and so enable those around us to become more fully human. May we ever seek to engage with the world, its young people and young families, Amen.

A Framework for Spiritual Discipline

Today is the first Sunday in Lent when our thoughts turn to a Lenten discipline, to what we give up and to fasting. I have been following what is called the 5:2 diet. It was heralded as something innovative and ground breaking, though is in fact as old as the hills. Each week I fast for 2 days and eat normally for 5. Fasting means restricting a man to 600 calories and a woman to 500.

When a young boy at home, I well remember having a much lighter diet every Friday and always eating fish. I am also very conscious that fasting every week is built into the monastic discipline which has been with us since St Anthony took himself off to the desert in the third century. Fasting has always traditionally been a part of a Lenten discipline. Way back in the Old Testament Isaiah was writing about fasting and the way the people had misunderstood its objective. He corrects them saying what God expects:-

"Is not this the kind of fasting I have chosen:
to loose the chains of injustice
and untie the cords of the yoke,
to set the oppressed free
and break every yoke?
7 Is it not to share your food with the hungry
and to provide the poor wanderer with shelter—
when you see the naked, to clothe them,
and not to turn away from your own flesh and blood?
8 Then your light will break forth like the dawn,
and your healing will quickly appear;
then your righteousness[a] will go before you,
and the glory of the LORD will be your rear guard.
9 Then you will call, and the LORD will answer;
you will cry for help, and he will say: Here am I.

"If you do away with the yoke of oppression,
with the pointing finger and malicious talk,
10 and if you spend yourselves on behalf of the hungry
and satisfy the needs of the oppressed,
then your light will rise in the darkness,
and your night will become like the noonday.
11 The LORD will guide you always;
he will satisfy your needs in a sun-scorched land
and will strengthen your frame.
You will be like a well-watered garden,
like a spring whose waters never fail.

At the end of January 2014, I held a conversation with Rowan Williams until recently Archbishop of Canterbury and since then Master of Magdalene College. The occasion helped raise money for the National Forum for Spirituality and Mental Health. In the part of the conversation about Theology, the Archbishop referred to a *framework* in which to undertake theology and as a tool for living. It seems to me that a Lenten discipline provides a framework to help us prepare for Easter. It does, however, do much more than this because frameworks are important for children, for our own spirituality and for helping each of us to mature.

A framework for children is vital because it provides secure boundaries and consequently helps to make children feel safe.

Let me quote from 'Children learn what they live':-

'If a child lives with criticism, he learns to condemn.
If a child lives with hostility, he learns to fight.
If a child lives with ridicule, he learns to be shy.
If a child lives with shame, he learns to feel guilty.
If a child lives with tolerance, he learns to be patient.
If a child lives with encouragement, he learns confidence.

If a child lives with praise, he learns to appreciate.

If a child lives with fairness, he learns justice.

If a child lives with security, he learns faith.

If a child lives with approval, he learns to like himself.

If a child lives with acceptance and friendship, he learns to find love in the world.

If a child lives with spirituality, he learns to appreciate God.'

A framework is equally important for our own spiritual life which nourishes us on a daily basis. Central to that framework is regular daily prayer which gives God the opportunity to converse with us and us with Him. It is here we offer in prayer the needs of the world, of communities, of families, and of individuals. If you ever tell anyone that you are praying for them, they will, as a rule, thank you profusely and look a little surprised.

A framework is also important in our quest for maturity. It is only after we have a framework for daily living in place, that we can move on and be free to develop so that we truly can be made in the image of God. It is St Paul who reminds us that only through true obedience can we become free. This is another way of talking about a framework for living, for children and for maturity. There is no time like the present. Lent is upon us and Easter beckons. There is much to do.

Prayer

We pray for order in our lives and for your guidance in our quest for maturity and fulfilling in ourselves the image in which you created us. May we be always ready to follow a daily discipline of fasting and prayer and live within a framework of obedience to your will., Amen.

The Desert

The Lenten season began with these words :

Jesus was in the wilderness for forty days,
Tempted by Satan;
And he was with the wild
beasts; and the angels
waited on him.

Deserts are both strange and serious places, strange because paradoxically they harbour both life and death. Every continent throughout the world has its desert. In South America there is the Atacana; in North America the Arizona; in Asia the Gobi Desert; in Africa the Kalahari and Sahara deserts; in Australia the Great Sandy, Victoria and Simpson deserts; and in Asia again the Sinai Desert which played such an important part in the history of the Jewish people. Only recently I heard the Pennines described by our Diocesan Bishop as "the last desert in England".

The lesson to be learnt from the Jewish experience of the desert is that it is a place in which people discover their identity. When the Jewish people left Egypt, they were fleeing from slavery. After forty years in the desert under the leadership of Moses, they arrived at the Promised Land, no longer slaves but identified as the people of God.

Jesus too was driven by the Spirit into the wilderness not for forty years, but for forty days and, in those six weeks, Jesus learnt about himself—who he was, what lay ahead of him and the dawning realization of his true identity. Later St Mark wrote......

(Mark 8: 34)

He called the crowd with his disciples, and
said to them, if any want to become a
followers of mine, let them deny themselves,
take up their cross and follow me.

There is an important strand in Christianity—some have supposed it the ideal—which directs believers away from the world and into the seclusion of prayer, austere self-denial, and spiritual contemplation.

This way of life has been embodied by monks and friars.

Monasticism began in Egypt around the start of the fourth century. Its earliest hero was St Anthony, who died in 356, and its style was extremely ascetic. The aspirants to religious perfection went off into the desert, or dwelt among the caves and catacombs of cemeteries, or sometimes, even, in the tradition of Simon Stylites, they passed their lives on pillars. There has always been this element of detachment in the great world religions and it is a way of life marked by fasting, prayer, solitude, and poverty. Certainly the desert is a place of silence and solitude, of slowness and simplicity. All of these are elements necessary (in a negative sense) to a life of self-denial and (in a positive sense) to the search for personal identity and meaning. Self-denial and discovery of one's identity require solitude in an uncluttered environment where the pace of life is slow and one is deafened by silence.

Because deserts are arid and scorched by the sun, keeping alive is no easy task. It is all too easy to become shriveled, dried up and die. At the same time deserts are places abounding in life which we have glimpsed on our television screens through programmes about the natural world, pioneered particularly by people like David Attenborough. Vita Sackville-West captures both the death and the life of the desert in this verse from a poem entitled "The Greater Cats".

> Their kind across the desert range
> Where tulips spring from stones, Not
> knowing they will suffer change or
> vultures pick their bones.
> Their strength's eternal in their sight,
> They rule the terror of the night, They
> overtake the deer in flight,
> And in their arrogance they smite;
> But I am sage, if they are strong;
> Man's love is transient as his death is long.

Deserts then are important places. They are strange places where we are confronted with both life and death and they are places the Christian is bidden to visit. Deserts have played an important part in the Old Testament, in the New Testament and in the growth of monasticism. They are places of refreshment as well as self-examination—in a sense refreshment is one of the results of careful self-examination because the person's spirit is freed from old prejudices and trappings through the refining process of self- examination.

Five weeks and it is Easter with its rich promise of new and all embracing life. If you are fully to appreciate the meaning, the glory and the importance of Easter, then you have no choice during this Lenten period but to go to the desert to find a place of silence and solitude, slowness and simplicity and in the process seek to find yourself.

Prayer

May we always be ready to travel into the deserts of this world wherever they may be and there find our true selves.

We ask that we may learn how to live simply, fast and pray

and be ready to be transformed through the process of self examination. As we come close to life and death in the desert, we pray that your spirit will always be there to guide and direct us, Amen.

The Weather and a rule of Life

In Britain the commonest topic of conversation is the weather. This might be because our weather is so changeable and seasonal. We have become used to hearing the weather being the cause of problems i.e. the familiar excuses which are given to explain why the trains do not run on time. In autumn there are leaves on the lines. In winter we have the wrong sort of snow; and there are environmental factors beyond our control which result in airports being closed for days on end. Today we are only too well aware of the havoc, devastation and chaos caused by recent earthquakes and volcanoes and our prayers and thoughts go out to the many thousands of people who have lost their homes, their livelihoods and their lives.

Meteorology—the study of all that contributes to what we call the weather—has an almost statutory place in the media. Whether we are listening to radio or watching television always, as the news ends, we are given the weather forecast. There is a link in popular thought between the weather and religion and there are times when clergy are asked to "put in a word" for good weather. Brides' fathers will sometimes say—"Vicar you are the one to make sure the sun is shining on the wedding day". I wish!

Were we to have been living with Abraham in early Old Testament times the weather, light and darkness, heat and cold, indeed the whole environment would likewise have been a very common topic of conversation. However, the difference for the Hebrew people was that they believed that the whole of life was subject to God, that there was nothing outside his authority and orbit and that God's activity incorporated every part of their lives.

As we read in the Old Testament……

'And the Lord said to Abram,
after Lot was separated from him,
Lift up now your eyes, and look from the place where you are
northward, and southward, and eastward, and westward:
For all the land which thou see, I will give it to you,
and to your seed forever.'

If the crops failed, then this was all part of God's design. In fact, the land that Abraham was promised—the Promised Land—was a land described as one flowing with milk and honey. In Old Testament theology the whole of life was governed by God and the people were ever conscious of the closeness of God, the activity of God and the presence of God.

In our own society today many people do not give God a second thought. There are some who do not even give him a first thought. There are those who think about God and respond to his love on an occasional basis, like those who attend baptisms, weddings and funerals. Even among those who attend Church regularly are some people whose preference is, metaphorically speaking, to leave God in church. Where is the desire, the urge, the necessity to seek God's presence in the world, to draw attention to his activity and to be ever conscious of his abiding presence. Being conscious of God's presence and aware that the whole of our live is an offering to him is left to the very committed and sometimes to the professionals which is how the clergy are perceived. Clergy are the people paid to go to church and say their prayers; one implication of this is that their prayers are somehow more efficacious.

The notion of commitment to continuous prayer and a mindset which acknowledges that God is always present with us can so easily become the preserve of a very select group of people called the religious. We leave it to monks and nuns to make a continuous offering of life to God. At the same time this is not a state of mind that should be restricted to the religious. Go into any of our great cathedrals and abbeys and look up at the Norman barrel vaults and marvelous Gothic fan vaulting in the roofs and chancels. Think of the masons who built these glorious places and of the medieval monks who, for nearly five hundred years and more, lived and worshipped in these places. They kept alive and preserved the faith for generations to come including our own. Their daily routine of work and prayer, quietness and study allowed them to make a life of continuous offering to God. They had a rule of life which enabled them to be conscious of God's presence with them at all times. At the height of the monastic movement there were 40,000 monks in monasteries across Europe and Western Asia. Today their numbers are drastically reduced, yet they are still charged with keeping alive the rumour of God.

Thomas Cranmer, when he compiled the first English Prayer Book, went to great lengths to make the daily monastic offices available to everyone in the Church of England. He did this by reducing the seven monastic offices into the services which today we call Matins and Evensong. In churches throughout the land, clergy and a growing number of lay people continue this daily routine by meeting both morning and evening to say Matins and Evensong. This framework of prayer, Bible reading and the daily office provides what might be described as today's "religious" with a pattern for daily living and I think it is perhaps this more than anything else that I missed when I retired. Even though many people are not able to join in this daily routine, they will be saying their own prayers at home or on the way to work. Nevertheless everyone has the opportunity to come to the Eucharist whether on Sundays or during the week. It is in the Eucharist par excellence, where the offering of life is made. Here, more than anywhere else is where we become acutely conscious of the presence of God as we place on the altar all that we have and all that we are and all that we hope to be—in fact the whole of our lives. We are invited to make a whole offering to God each time we come to Communion. Pray for a sense of wholeness in all we do so that we can ever celebrate the work of God in the world.

Help us, Lord, always to recognize and acknowledge your presence in the natural world. May we celebrate your guidance through our lives and the presence of your spirit within each of us. Encourage us to live a life of prayer and always be ready to meet you in the breaking of bread and sharing of wine. Nourished by the food and drink of life eternal, may we ever be a source of nourishment to those we seek to serve, Amen.

Mothers

A saying you will often hear is "Motherhood and apple pie". It is used about discussions and situations which are thought to be non-controversial, non-political and with outcomes with which we can all agree. "Motherhood and apple pie" refer not to things which are hard and difficult but soft and manageable. I am not so sure about this, especially if you have tasted my apple pie! To create the right texture and colour in the pastry which tops the apple pie and introduce exactly the right flavour of nutmeg and other ingredients is an art form. Ironically when it is successful, the cry goes up "just like mother used to make". One of my objectives (seldom realized) has been to improve my cooking skills and recently I asked Melanie, who is an ace cook, how to make pastry. To my surprise she said probably the easiest thing is to go and buy pastry already made at the local supermarket. So much for apple pie, but what about motherhood and is it uncontroversial or non political and something about which everyone can agree? I really do have my doubts. Motherhood encompasses a wide group of people viz.

Mothers
Grandmothers
Surrogate mothers
Stepmothers
Foster mothers
Adoptive mothers
Godmothers

At the heart of motherhood is that ability to turn a house into a home where families and children can be nurtured. I never cease to be amazed how quickly this can happen. After moving to a new house and before the unpacking begins, suddenly mother has conjured up a meal from seemingly nowhere. Think for a moment of Jesus' childhood. Mary, his mother, had created a nursery in a stable and then a home above a carpenter's shop. Later, when he was about twelve years old, she was to experience that awful fear and terror when he went missing. He was found talking to the academics in the temple. Today, when a child goes missing, it frequently happens that sadly there is not a happy ending. Think of the children to whom this has happened recently and about whom nothing further has been heard or the most awful situations that were uncovered in the London borough of Haringey and the Northern town of Dewsbury and Doncaster and more recently in other places.

Motherhood involves creating a home, nurturing the family, providing an environment of love, and ensuring security and safety. All of these are absolutely vital for growing up into adulthood in the society in which we live. There is a crying need to ensure the continuity of family and community life and perhaps one of the few organisations best placed to enhance family and community living is the church. The church calls itself a family, calls itself mother church and seeks to establish a Christian community which is open to everyone regardless of who they are or where they come from. The church building can only function in any real sense if the doors are open. I well remember one summer's day when, at the beginning of the Sunday morning service, the doors which had been left wide open to let in the people and the sunlight, were then closed by the churchwarden. Why, I asked, had he done this? To which I received the perverse reply—now that you are about to begin the service, we do not want anybody else coming in. When it is warm enough, church doors should be left open and, as an Archdeacon, I regularly encouraged parishes to make the main church doors of glass. There is a fine example in the parish of St Wulfram, Grantham of a lovely glass porch which has won prizes on the inside of the great west door which, even when the church is locked, allows the passerby to look into the interior of this wonderful building. It is time for the church—both people and buildings—once again to become central to the life of the local community. The church needs to be vibrant and outward looking, socially responsible and daring to be political. It is only then it will be able to promote community living and family values. I am encouraged by two things. The first is the amount of goodwill towards the church which continues to exist in parishes, especially rural parishes. Secondly I am always amazed by the range of responsibilities that regular church people undertake. I remember asking a local PCC whether it thought the parish council would agree to its request, only to be told—'no problem, half the parish council are on the PCC anyway.' Promoting community and family life have their origins in the home, where motherhood finds its best expression. It is interesting that we always refer to the homeless, not the houseless. Those who are homeless obviously need a roof over their head, but very quickly they need that roof to change into a home.

Being a mother and living out motherhood can at times be tested to the extremes. When a child is lost, when a child is homeless, when a child is disabled and needs long-term care, all can test motherhood; nor is this testing confined to what may happen to children. I am thinking of a secure prison I know well where there are over three hundred women, many of whom are serving long sentences, usually for being in possession of illegal drugs. Many of these women are mothers who during their imprisonment cannot be mothers, cannot exercise motherhood and have to rely upon others to fulfil that role. When visiting the prison, the chaplain told me that some of the women will never be allowed to be mothers again because their children have already been adopted and the mothers are then denied access to the children.

Motherhood is, I repeat, about nurturing and loving and also about being able to let go. It is what Melanie calls holding them tightly with loose hands and giving them roots and wings. So much depends upon early childhood experiences which shape and influence the child. These include their value systems, their spirituality and how they will come to understand being a child of God. Let me finish with some words that are entitled "Children Learn What They Live".

If a child lives with criticism, he learns to condemn.
If a child lives with hostility, he learns to fight.
If a child lives with ridicule, he learns to be shy.
If a child lives with shame, he learns to feel guilty.
If a child lives with tolerance, he learns to be patient.
If a child lives with encouragement, he learns confidence.
If a child lives with praise, he learns to appreciate.
If a child lives with fairness, he learns justice.
If a child lives with security, he learns faith.
If a child lives with approval, he learns to like himself.
If a child lives with acceptance and friendship, he learns to find love in the world.
If a child lives with spirituality, he learns to appreciate God.

Prayer
Thank you, good Lord, for our mothers and all that they do for us. May the world ever celebrate mothers and the church be a family which is a vehicle of nurture, love and nourishment. May your Spirit always be present with those mothers who suffer and make sacrifices for their children and families, Amen.

The Story of Atonement

Chapter five of one of the previous reports of the Doctrine Commission of the Church of England carried the title 'Retelling the Story' which is the story of the mystery of salvation. This particular chapter uses another word in place of the word 'salvation'. It talks about 'atonement' and this is because the chapter deals with the way in which salvation is worked out through the activity of Jesus and, most particularly, his death on the cross. I would like to consider briefly the different ways in which atonement has been understood, the situation the story is addressing, what it means to follow the way of the cross and, finally, why it is important to tell stories in the first place.

There are various theories of the atonement. The word has to do with the activity of atoning, helping to put things right, perhaps not just once but many times. Introduce two hyphens into the word the meaning changes to 'at-one-ment'. At-one -ment stresses much more the activity of reconciliation, of bringing people to God so that the two become one. This idea is given a particular expression in the Eucharist where, by sharing in the bread which is distributed to the people of God we are united in the body of Christ. The idea is captured by St Paul when, in a sentence, he explains the mystery of salvation— 'God was in Christ reconciling the world to himself'. The first theory of the atonement is that of sacrifice and one of the Easter anthems expresses this very clearly—'Christ, our Passover is sacrificed for us, therefore, let us keep the feast'. Jesus himself is seen as a sacrifice to God for the sins of humanity. Much of the thinking is dependent upon Old Testament theology and the use of sacrifice in the history of the Hebrew people.

The second theory of atonement comes from the writings of St Anselm and is called the 'Theory of Satisfaction'. Again, we come across this in the Communion service in the Book of

Common Prayer where we read that 'Jesus' suffering and death were an oblation and satisfaction for the sins of the whole world.

The third theory developed at the time of the Reformation stresses Jesus' death being understood more in legalistic terms, in the sense that Jesus' death saves humanity from eternal punishment.

The fourth theory is about victory and links the cross with the resurrection and here Jesus' death and resurrection are understood as life overcoming death. It is St Paul who says "Death has been swallowed up in victory. Where, O Death, is your victory?"

The last theory of the atonement is often called the 'Moral' theory and was first given prominence by Peter Abelard. He understood Jesus' death on the cross to be an example of an unparalleled expression of the love of God. On the one hand Jesus perfectly displays the compassionate love of God for estranged humanity. On the other hand, his outpoured love on the cross awakens in us a corresponding penitence, faith, love and obedience. This idea speaks much more of the reconciliation that I was mentioning earlier and lends itself more to the radical shift which we have seen this century in our understanding of the nature of God.

Today, thanks to people like Bonhoeffer and Hans Kung on the Continent and Bill Vanstone ('Love's Endeavour, Love's Expense') in our own country, we are much more ready to understand God as suffering with us. How else can we make sense of the problem of unmerited or disproportionate suffering? This theology of the reconciliation of humanity to God through God's bearing of human pain (as well as human sin) has emerged from the massive experience of affliction in the 20th century, says the report—'The Mystery of Salvation'— from the trenches of the First World War to the extermination camps in Nazi Europe; and from our deepest awareness of the darkness of mental illness to our growing realization of the innumerable ways in which women have been exploited and oppressed and recently the re-emergence of slavery. The gathering conviction that 'only the suffering God can help' has led to widespread questioning of the traditional assumption that the divine nature cannot enter into or share human experience, especially suffering. The situation the Christian story, the Gospel message, addresses is the way in which God deals with our human situation. It is really about how God relates to us and how we relate to him and it means following the way of the cross. The way of the cross picks up that idea which I mentioned of sacrifice. It means that there are no short cuts and, in the words of last week's Collect, there is pain before joy and crucifixion before glory.

Furthermore, the way of the cross brings scapegoating to an end. One way of dealing with sin in the Old Testament was to project it quite literally onto some poor unsuspecting goat that was then driven into the wilderness. The point about Jesus' death is simply that he did not look for a scapegoat. Certainly, Simon of Cyrene helped to carry the cross but it was Jesus who died on it. There was no attempt to involve anyone or anything else but rather to contain sin within himself. This is a major difference in the theology of the Old Testament and the theology of the New Testament.

Scapegoating ends. You have to live with your own backyard however great the temptation to put everything into somebody else's.

Lastly, the cross gives the lie to that all too familiar human desire to be divisive and to split good from bad, pain from glory and the cross from resurrection. The whole point of treating Good Friday and Easter Day as a whole, of incorporating the suffering into the glory and the cross into the resurrection is to avoid the possibility of introducing divisions and splits.

Jesus held the whole situation together and brought a unity and purpose to the pain that he suffered which is what we know as the process of reconciliation.

One way of continuing this work of reconciliation between God and people and people with each other is to continue to tell the story. It echoes the title of chapter five—retelling the story. Our task is to find every possible means and explore every available way to tell the story again and again. In essence, it means preaching the Gospel. But, let me finish by quoting a passage from a chapter I wrote in a book published just before Christmas. I had been talking about the importance of people repeating their story when they are in a counselling situation with particular reference to people who are bereaved.

"The repeating of the person's story is not only an important element within psychotherapy but also within the natural process of bereavement itself and it is this conversation repeated over and over again that offers the possibility of rehabilitation for the sufferer. The test for such a robust statement is to be found among those people who, for reasons beyond their control, have no story to tell. I remember well the situation a colleague once explained to me. Her family had grown up and one of her sons remained single and lived a very carefree life in which he would set out in his sailing boat often going across the Channel to France and further afield to the Mediterranean, the North African coast and the Near East.

He would moor his boat, work a while to earn money for food and then set off to his next destination. He would always drop a card home telling his parents where he was and where he expected to be next. One day he waved goodbye to his mother and set off on another voyage. Since he left she has received no postcard and no communication of his whereabouts and that was twelve years ago. The conclusion his parents have naturally reached is that he is missing presumed dead. Now they have no story to tell and no fixed point. There is no body to identify and no hard evidence indicating death. The result is that they cannot begin to grieve, even though they know in their hearts that he is dead through one cause or another. It is as though they live in suspended animation, or in a state of limbo. This illustration demonstrates the essential need for everyone to have a story to tell."

Telling the story and retelling the story is absolutely vital. I will end where most stories begin which is...

"Once upon a time when the great Israel Baal Shem Tov saw misfortune threatening the Jews, it was his custom to go into a certain part of the forest to meditate. There he would light a fire, say a special prayer, and the miracle would be accomplished and the misfortune averted. Later, when his disciple, the celebrated Maggid of Mezeritch, had occasion, for the same reason, to intercede with heaven, he would go to the same place in the forest and say: 'Master of the Universe, listen! I do not know how to light the fire but I am still able to say the prayer.' And again the miracle would be accomplished.

Still later, Moshe-Leib of Sassov, in order to save his people once more, would go into the forest and say: 'I do not know the prayer, but I know the place and this must be sufficient.' It was sufficient and the miracle was accomplished.

Then it fell to Israel of Rizhin to overcome misfortune. Sitting in his armchair, his head in his hands, he spoke to God: 'I am unable to light the fire and I do not know the prayer; I cannot even find the place in the forest. All I can do is tell the story, and this must be sufficient.' And it was sufficient."

Prayer

God, our Father, thank you for sending your Son to atone for the sins of humanity. May we be caught up in the activity of atonement to become one with you in Christ. Give us, we pray, the confidence to tell the story again and again in our time so that others may come to know and understand your activity in Jesus, Amen.

Colours of the Cross

Today is often referred to as 'Passion Sunday' and, naturally, our thoughts turn to the cross which has a central place in the worship of the church, particularly in the next two weeks .

I believe the cross plays a central part in christian theology and in the practical expression of the christian faith. Of course, as the vehicle of our redemption it is always prominent in christian life and liturgy. There are innumerable misunderstandings and sometimes ignorance about the cross among many people.

Something I learned about baptising children from a Roman Catholic priest was to invite parents to put their thumb into the water in the font and make the sign of the cross with the water on their child's forehead. I do sometimes wonder what is going through their minds and what they think it means and represents. You may have heard the story of someone who went into a shop to purchase a crucifix. The shop assistant said that there were two sorts of crosses, one was plain and the other had a little man on it!

There are, indeed, many ways (and no ways) to think about the cross. These last weeks we have concentrated on the crosses people have had to bear in the Middle East, particularly Syria. These crosses and scars they will carry for the rest of their lives.

Let us, for a moment, concentrate on the ways in which each of the four Gospels present the cross, recognising from the outset that they are different and that each evangelist has his own particular way of treating the Passion material. The Gospels of Matthew, Mark, Luke and John do not just vary in style but also in the way the writers handle the facts at their disposal. St Matthew's Gospel is a history book, a teaching gospel, and it is often the favourite gospel for reading aloud in church. It contains that great body of teaching called the Sermon on the Mount and we read at the beginning of it that Jesus sat down to teach the people in the tradition of the rabbis. The crowd of people gathered round him, sitting on the green slopes of the hillside. The cross in St Matthew's Gospel is a pulpit from which the message of salvation is preached, first to the Jewish people and then to the whole of mankind. Perhaps the colour of this cross is green which is the colour marking the time of the liturgical year when the preacher is freer to choose the theme of the sermon, especially during the summer months when none of the great festivals occur.

St Mark's Gospel is altogether different. It is journalistic. There is a short snappy introduction, no Christmas stories and then the narrative moves straight into the main events of Jesus' life through a series of small stories which contribute to the greater story. As with the other Gospels, a third of St Mark is devoted to the last week of Jesus' life. St Mark's cross is black and sombre. It is a gallows on which Jesus died and St Mark is at pains to show that Jesus really did die. It was the centurion standing at the foot of the cross who, as Jesus died, said "Truly that man was a son of God".

St Luke is different again. His Gospel has a lyrical style. He, more than all the others, emphasises the role of women in the life of Jesus. Without St Luke's Gospel we would not have the account of Mary visiting John the Baptist's mother, Elizabeth, or the Magnificat, or the delightful tale about old Anna who, like Simeon, identified the young child as the Christ or the description of the women who were with Jesus as he made his way from the city of Jerusalem to Calvary. As in the other Gospels, the way in which the cross is presented reflects the central theme of the Gospel and I believe the cross in St Luke's Gospel is a mercy seat. The cross becomes a vehicle of God's mercy and it is to the cross that we come to seek God's forgiveness, his acceptance and mercy—for we know that we only receive forgiveness from

God because he is merciful. The colour of the Lukan cross

is blue which is the colour associated with Mary who, in the christian tradition, is the epitome of womanhood.

Lastly, we turn to the fourth Gospel which varies quite markedly from the other three. Its literary style is mystical. As with St Mark's Gospel there are no nativity stories but rather atheological treatise on Jesus' divine origins. Before the second chapter ends there is already reference to his death which is pre-empted again and again as the Gospel unfolds. In fact the cross is the last of the signs John uses to reveal the glory of Jesus, the son of God. In St John's scheme of things the cross is a vehicle of glory. It is a means by which God's glory is revealed in Jesus and it becomes a throne on which the King of Glory is crowned.

As well as having a plain cross and a cross with a little man on it, there is also what is called the 'Christus Rex'. This is a cross on which the figure of Jesus is clothed and crowned. It is a way of expressing his glory and kingship. The colour of this cross is white. As the body of Jesus is lifted up on the cross so the King of glory is lifted up, rooted in this earth and at the same time drawn up into the Godhead. Even though St John records for us an account of the resurrection there is a sense in which for him Jesus' crucifixion is also his resurrection.

The nuns at East Grinstead expressed this particular understanding of Jesus' death and resurrection in their Good Friday liturgies.They move away from temporal realism which describes the events of Holy Week in a systematic way where death is followed by burial and burial by resurrection. They choose what is called dynamic realism where cross and resurrection are brought together in one explosive event. Their first Eucharist of Easter takes place on the night of Good Friday!

Here, then, are four possible ways of approaching the cross. It is a Green pulpit, a black gallows, a blue mercy seat and a white throne. In fact these four colours are the colours of the horses of the apocalypse in the book of Revelation (Chapter 6 vs. 1 to

8) As you make your way through Passion Week and the events of Holy Week, you are encouraged to take up your cross and to follow him. Your image of the cross may change as you receive new insights into the meaning of Christ's passion, his death and resurrection and how it affects you.

Our common prayer is that each of us will stand at the foot of the cross and be ready to be changed by it and so participate in a new way in the glory and the promise of resurrection.

Prayer

We pray that we will always ensure the cross is at the centre of our devotional life. Help us, good Lord, to understand the myriad meanings of the cross on which the Saviour wrought the redemption of the world. As he was lifted up into glory, may we too be lifted up in to your eternal presence, Amen.

Christ the King

(Jeremiah 23 v 5-6)
The days are now coming, says the Lord,
when I will make a righteous Branch spring from David's line,
a king who shall rule wisely,
maintaining law and justice in the land.
In his days Judah shall be kept safe,
and Israel shall live undisturbed.
This is the name to be given to him:
The Lord is our Righteousness.

Having expectations is part of being human. It is also part of what it is to be a Christian. Expectations are about the future, about waiting upon God and waiting is one way in which we attend to our inner spiritual life. It is here that we wait patiently to hear the still small voice of God, where we wait with expectation to understand ourselves better as slowly but surely, we pray, we may continually be reshaped and recrafted in the image of God.

Groups of people and nations can have expectations. The Jews, after their exile, expected to return to their own homeland, to re-establish the kingdom of David and to welcome a new king. The Lord, in the words of the text from Jeremiah, accedes to their prayers and promises to raise up a king who will follow in the line of David. He will satisfy their longings and meet their expectations and will be called "the Lord is our righteousness".

It was just this sort of king that the people of Jerusalem were expecting on the first Palm Sunday when Jesus arrived at the gates of Jerusalem. They could not have been more mistaken. The people who lined the route hailed the anointed one to be their King. Jesus was indeed a king. He was a king who acted wisely, executed justice and righteousness, but he was not the type of king that everyone had been expecting. Let us spend a moment looking at Jesus' trappings of kingship which are so clearly displayed when he entered the city of Jerusalem.

He did not arrive at the gates of Jerusalem at speed in a chariot pulled by a white charger but riding a donkey. The same animal was present at his birth and provided a means of transport for Mary, when she and Joseph escaped the hands of Herod with the young child. Etched along the back and shoulders of every donkey in a darker colour is the outline of a cross—another symbol of Jesus' kingship. As the donkey with its sacred burden approached the gates of the city, Jesus was not greeted by a flag waving crowd but by people who had pulled branches from the trees as they chorused, "Blessed is the one who comes in the name of the Lord—the King of Israel". It had already been written that the people were not to be afraid because, look, your king is coming, sitting on the foal of a donkey.

When he was hailed as a king arraigned before his accusers, his coronation robes were not of gold and ermine, but a tunic borrowed from a nearby soldier. Nor was his crown studded with jewels set in a gold band like the one worn by Herod, one of his inquisitors. His crown was woven from the long sharp thorns taken from the thorn bushes that predominated in Palestine. The crown was forced down on to his brow so that the thorns lacerated his head and the blood flowed down his face and dropped from his chin.

He did not carry an orb or sceptre as was the tradition with kings and emperors. No, he held a reed and the orb was a sponge soaked in wine vinegar, a crude attempt to allay his parched throat. The throne on which Jesus was crowned as king was not one passed from dynasty to dynasty resting on a platform in the throne room of a king's palace. Jesus was forced to carry his own throne—a cross which was set upon a green hill outside the city walls where the town dumped its rubbish.

In the fourth Gospel, St John makes it abundantly clear that the cross is the sign of salvation. It is the vehicle by which Jesus is lifted up into glory. It is the throne on which Jesus is crowned as King of Heaven. Though hewn from dark wood, it shines with a brightness when the betrayed son of God is crucified between two robbers.

This is the king who was welcomed into Jerusalem on that first Palm Sunday. He was a king who washed people's feet, who spent time with those whom society had rejected, with outcasts and lepers [today those who suffer with HIV/Aids] those who inhabited the edges and fringes of society, those who lived in dark and twilight areas, those who were going nowhere; where he died was a metaphor for those to whom he ministered.

Our king, Christ the king of glory, the king of peace, turned people's thinking and values upside down. He did not meet their expectations, rather he challenged their presuppositions, asked them to look again at themselves and deepen their understanding of the God they worshipped. He turned their world upside down and his throne, the cross, became a stumbling block for the Jews and folly to the Greeks.

It is never easy for institutions to change and be innovative and this is for two reasons. Firstly institutions are almost by definition protective and seek to sustain subtle and sensitive balances between the inner life of the organisation and the world outside. Secondly there are usually power games being played where first one person or group and then another bid for control. Neither of these fit the style of Jesus and the Gospel. Jesus focused on our inner life, on what makes us tick, on the divine spark and his only interest in the world was to save and serve it. As for power politics, he turned them upside down and was critical and scathing about the leaders of his time; those, who, in turn, pursued him to his death. Hard as it may be institutions do have to change and the church is no exception. The church needs to change but only for one reason and it is to be better equipped to live and speak the Gospel in our own generation. This does mean being, as they say, counter-cultural. It does mean challenging the self-centeredness of the age in which we live. It does mean questioning endless choice. It does mean doing everything possible to lessen the gap between the "haves" and "have-nots". It does mean expressing the love, justice and glory of God in the world in which we live. It does mean being good stewards of all that we are given including the planet on which we live. It does mean looking carefully at our own resources—the people we have, the buildings we have inherited and the tradition and heritage of our faith. It does mean following in the steps of Jesus. We are invited to join the crowds at the gates of Jerusalem and follow the road that leads through the city out to the green hill and finally to the garden where we find an empty tomb and the hope of resurrection. Resurrection is a celebration of the other side of ourselves. This is a side that God sees and this is a side which is the gateway to eternity. Here we can step into the very presence of God himself where we celebrate a beginning, not an end. It is here, believe me, that Christ the king reigns supreme.

Prayer

Thank you for our king, Christ the king of glory, Christ the king of peace, who turned people's thinking and values upside down. He challenged the presuppositions of his listeners and asked them to look again at themselves and deepen their understanding of the God they worshipped. We pray that he will, in the same way, challenge us so that we might enrich our inner lives and better serve the world, Amen.

Easter

(St Matthew 28 verses 6–10)

"I know you are looking for Jesus who was crucified. He is not here; he has been raised again, as he said he would be. Come and see the place where he was laid, and then go quickly and tell his disciples: 'He has been raised from the dead and he is going on before you into Galilee; there you will see him'. That is what I had to tell you.

They hurried away from the tomb in awe and great joy, and ran to tell the disciples. Suddenly Jesus was there in their path. He gave them his greeting, and they came up and clasped his feet, falling prostrate before him. Then Jesus said to them, "Do not be afraid. Go and take the word to my brothers that they are to leave for Galilee. They will see me there."

Today is Easter Day which begins by celebrating an empty tomb but far more than an empty tomb. There is a book with the title "Who moved the stone?" It remains a question today about how the huge stone which sealed the tomb was moved to enable Jesus to break through the shackles of death in order to be able to walk into new life. This belief of new life in Christ is at the heart of our Christian faith which we proclaim every time we meet in church and say the creed. We say that we believe in "the resurrection of the body and the life everlasting". Why then do we need a belief in a bodily resurrection—whether we are thinking of St Paul's version of a resurrected body which could appear in rooms with locked doors or whether something else? The first reason is consistency, consistency with the rest of Jesus' life. We believe that he was born as a real baby with a real mother in a real place which you can visit today. There are those who think that Jesus was not a real person but that he was what you might call a "spiritual shadow". Whatever we do, let us not "spiritualise" either Jesus' birth or resurrection. Otherwise we shall replace our belief in the resurrection of the body with a belief in the immortality of the soul which is very post modern with its definition of spirituality that "it does not matter what you believe, as long as what you believe does not matter". It is this belief that lies behind the increasing number of requests that I received, as an Archdeacon, for permission to remove the cremated remains of a husband or wife, when people move house.

The second reason we believe in the resurrection of the body is to do with how we identify each other. Unless we have bodies how else are we to identify people in heaven? Bodies are important because they contain our experiences, they portray our characteristics, they express our personalities, and they shelter our inner life. In my view it has long been a mistake to separate body and spirit. Rather we must hold them together in a dynamic and creative tension.

Thirdly we know that the church itself is given the description "the body of Christ". Not only is this body, the church, itself an expression of the resurrection, but it is also a real body with real people. In the body of Christ there are experiences contained and characteristics portrayed. Personalities are expressed and the inner life with God is fed and nurtured. A bodily resurrection is then essential to Christian belief. It was Christ's body that broke out of the tomb into another dimension, into a total experience of God and into eternity. A tomb hewn out of a cave in Joseph's garden could not contain almighty God. Resurrection, is then, about "breaking through".

We mirror breaking through in our own lives and in our own personal experiences. You will know how relationships mature and how in the closeness of two people the process of maturity is brought about by breaking through the different layers of the relationship; rather like peeling back the layers of an onion. It does take a long time and sometimes people who have been together for twenty years or more, say that they would not have believed that there was another dimension to their relationship. Yet they gain new insights, broaden their horizons, taste a new way of living and suddenly—yes suddenly—they break through into a new experience of relating. This is resurrection at work in personal experience and in human relationships.

After Jesus' resurrection, the women wondered where they would see him and the angel said "Go to Galilee". Alternatively the angel might have said join Jesus on the road to Emmaus or celebrate new life when a baby is born or give thanks to God for an act of grace or meet the risen Christ in the sacrament of bread and wine or see hands at work when a sick person is anointed or experience resurrection every time you break through. Every time you break through you enter deeper into holiness and glory and deeper into the mystery of God himself.

Celebrate Easter, enjoy resurrection and break through into new life and new horizons.

Prayer

We celebrate resurrection in all its wonder, complexity and simplicity. Thank you, good Lord, for your promise of new life in the resurrected Jesus. We pray for new horizons and new possibilities in the lives of all people, so that they are able to break through and enter deeper into holiness and glory and further into Your mystery, Amen.

Easter Day

(John 12 verse 24)
Unless a grain of wheat falls on
the ground and dies, it remains a
single grain; but, if it dies, it yields a rich harvest.

The humble potato is synonomous with Norfolk. Being the good traditionalists that you are I am sure you followed that age old tradition of planting your seed potatoes on Good Friday.

Towards the end of the spring you will be able to dig up the roots and gather small fresh new potatoes which, with a sprig of mint and a pat of butter, will taste better than anything you can buy in the supermarket or at the vegetable store. This is because the potatoes will be absolutely fresh and also because they will have come from your garden and it will have been your work that nurtured them. As you dig up the first root of potatoes your fork may sink into the now dead seed potato. If you pick it up with your hand, it is likely that the soft, dead, mushy inside of the potato will squirt all over you. You quickly discard the now dead seed potato and concentrate on the new ones growing in abundance on the root. The potato which first arrived on these shores from America and has now become part of the staple diet of this country—where on earth would we be without chips—is a metaphor for Easter.

In a sentence there is no new life unless the old life has ended. Unless a grain of wheat falls into the ground and dies or unless a seed potato becomes mushy and dies, there will be no new growth. Death precedes resurrection just as Good Friday precedes Easter Day. Easter Day cannot stand on its own but always has to follow Good Friday. Of course, it is also true that without the possibility of resurrection there is only death; the grain of wheat remains a single grain. It is then the more surprising to find in churches up and down the country many more people attending services on Easter Day than do so on Good Friday. The lesson of the seed potato is that there is no short cut and this is a lesson to be learned by the church and also by the society in which we live. The call to be entrepreneurial so often becomes no more than a way of finding short cuts.

Death has, then, to be confronted and lived with, if there is to be resurrection, if there is to be hope and if there is to be new life. This is by no means a sad or depressing thought but rather a cause for great celebration. I remember a contemporary of mine at theological college who, on the first Easter Day in his first parish, stepped into the pulpit with his sermon notes in his hand. He looked around him and then said that he had spent a long time preparing a sermon to preach to them all but he was not going to preach it. This was because they all looked so terribly unhappy and downcast. Instead he shouted aloud 'Jesus Christ is risen, Alelluia' . He then tore up his notes and threw all the little pieces of paper over the congregation. He then left the pulpit and began the words of the Nicene Creed. Nobody in church on that Easter Day ever forgot the sermon! It was a reminder that Easter is a joyful festival, a time of celebration and a day when we offer thanks to God for all that he did in Jesus.

There are, of course, Good Fridays in contemporary society and there are modern Easter Days. There are those who are called upon to cope with death in their families and among their friends, there are those who face death themselves and there are also other types of loss—what I call little deaths. Increasingly in modern society there are areas where there is no longer any sense of community, where we expect people to live and work in harmony with one another, to be neighbourly and have a care for each other. Community life in some areas has completely died. Where community life has broken down, there are those who are victims of violence. A once confident and outgoing person becomes timid and anxious, withdrawn and frightened. The liveliness that they once had seems to have gone for ever. There are also those who have had to learn somehow to live their lives without ever engaging in full time paid employment. They are branded failures by others more fortunate and find it incredibly difficult to give any sort of structure to their lives, any meaning and, consequently, to feel that they are in any way valued.

The days of the availability of work for everyone have long since gone. There are so many losses that people face before being confronted with death itself. There is redundancy, divorce, retirement, the loss of good health, the loss of friends there are so many human situations in which people are confronted with loss. All of these feel like a cross to bear, each one is like a little Good Friday. The message of Easter is that, in the face of loss, we have hope. This is because we believe that God acted in such a way that what was once unbelievable becomes believable and I am not just referring to resurrection or, indeed, to the resurrection of the body but rather the improbability of the Gospel itself. What was unbelievable but is now believable; in the words of St Paul 'God was in Christ reconciling the world to himself'. This surely is the greatest mystery that in Jesus we see the activity of God, in the human we see the divine, in the improbable we see the possible, in despair we see hope and, in the words of St Francis of Assisi, *In hatred we see love, in injury we see pardon, in doubt we see faith, in darkness we see light and in sadness we see joy'.* Easter, then, offers us a future and, as we begin to delve into its mystery and unpack its meaning in the weeks to come, the resurrection appearances of Jesus will remind us of his abiding presence, the events in the house at Emmaus will reassure us that we never walk alone and the empty tomb will encourage us to believe the unbelievable.

Three Gardens

At the turn of the century Dorothy Gurney wrote these words:-

> 'The kiss of the sun for pardon,
> The song of the birds for mirth
> One is nearer God's heart in a garden
> Than anywhere else on earth`.

There are three gardens which feature prominently in God's economy and our salvation. Come with me for a moment, if you will, and we shall visit each of them.

The first is the Garden of Eden, mythologically situated in what was once called Mesopotamia—that strange and exotic land between the river Euphrates and Tigris. Today we call the country Iraq. It has been and remains very much in our prayers, after all the recent troubles.

Here was a garden paradise full of fruiting trees, colourful flowers and shrubs and, in the centre, was one tree—the Tree of Knowledge—the fruit of which the garden creatures were forbidden to taste. The inhabitants were called Man and Woman, or in Hebrew Adam and Eve. By disobeying the rule for life in the garden and by eating forbidden fruit, Adam and Eve consumed knowledge. As a consequence they were able to choose and to distinguish right from wrong and so lost the innocence they had enjoyed in the garden paradise. The Garden of Eden is the garden of creation; it is here that we are offered a microcosm of what I always think of as the first wonder of the world, which is the created universe itself. From this point onwards human beings were able to choose whether to co-operate in the activity of creation or to rebel against it. Central to the tenets of the Christian faith is the realisation that in the person of Jesus, in what he said and did we are offered a new way of making choices. This way is not dependent upon rules, regulations and laws but on love, particularly at those points where human love responds to divine love. The gospel of love was worked out to its conclusion in Jesus' own life; so it is that we find ourselves being invited to walk in another garden.

This is the Garden of Gethsemane to which Jesus retired after the last supper he had eaten with his friends. They were still confused by some of the things he had said about the bread and his body and the wine that they were drinking and doing this in remembrance of him. They were still alarmed by the sudden and unexplained disappearance of Judas and they felt not a little drowsy after good food and plenty of strong eastern Mediterranean wine. They fell asleep and so did not witness the struggle which confronted Jesus that night.

Jesus' spirit and God's intentions for humanity were laid bare. In this garden Jesus wrestled with the enormity of the task that lay ahead of him. The possible futility of his death tested his faith to the extreme. Alone in the garden he made his decision. He surrendered into the hands of wicked men and was taken away to be tried and executed. It was an act of faith. There were no guarantees, no proof of resurrection and no assurance of success. I believe that when Jesus left the garden with the soldiers, he stepped out into the unknown—as we say today, a leap of faith.

The third garden was the one which belonged to Joseph of Arimathea. It is the garden we call the Garden of Resurrection and it was here that Mary mistook Jesus for the gardener, until He quietly spoke her name—Mary—then she ran as fast as she could to tell the other apostles what had happened. The poem indicated that we are nearer God's heart in a garden than anywhere else on earth. It is certainly true that some of the central tenants of our Christian faith are to be found acted out in gardens.

T.S. Eliot writes in one of his four Quartets ......

To be conscious is not to be in time
But only in time can the moment in the rose-garden,
The moment in the arbour where the rain beat,
The moment in the draughty church at smokefall
Be remembered; involved with past and future.
Only through time, time is conquered.

These are three gardens which remind us of creation, of redemption and resurrection—three gardens which help us to understand better how God works with us, how the cross is a vehicle of love, a throne on which the King of glory is crowned and how Gethsemane changes into Resurrection.

Central to the Easter Faith is the promise of new life which is why we have Easter eggs and Easter rabbits. From the egg-shaped Easter tomb emerges the promise of moving ever deeper into the mystery of God and the mystery of each other. This is what I call the Heineken factor. It offers the possibility of going where we have never been before, to parts still unexplored and to the very heart of our own mystery. 'We shall not cease from exploration and (says Eliot) the end of all our exploring will be to arrive where we started and know the place for the first time.'

One Easter hymn has the words ... 'now is the eternal life, if risen with Christ we stand'. There is not a moment to lose if the kingdom of God is to grow and people are to be convinced that Christ is risen, God is real and alive in everyone.

Prayer
    Lord God we celebrate the earth you have placed in our care and pray that we may ever rise to the challenge to sustain it. We believe our creation, redemption and new life were completed in three gardens. Bless each of us, we pray, as we enter this new life of hope and glory, Amen.

Resurrection Pictures

I wonder what pictures you have in your mind of Jesus' resurrection. I have had the privilege of spending Lent, Holy Week and Easter in a parish in the city (of Lincoln). I was particularly grateful to the incumbent who invited me to celebrate and preach at the main service on Easter Day. I wonder how many clergy would be happy for another priest to celebrate at the main Eucharistic service on the most important day in the Christian calendar! Though a priest, I do not have a parish but responsibility for 288 parishes in the Archdeaconry of Lincoln. Doing this strange job means that I have neither altar nor community and so it was a wonderful Easter present to be offered both. One of the groups in the parish met on Wednesday evenings in Lent and was looking at the role of the local church as it seeks to support and serve the local community. There were long discussions about what this word "local" might mean, though I cannot remember anybody thinking it referred to the pub! The last time the group met it was asked to prepare a display in the Museum of Lincolnshire Life which depicted both the local Christian church and also the meaning of Easter. It is not easy to create a physical, visual, tangible portrayal of Easter. Eventually it was decided to usewords like "Jesus is risen", but then words are limited because they are two-dimensional rather than three-dimensional.

So what pictures do you have in your mind? Perhaps it is the empty tomb out of which Jesus rose from the dead. On the other hand, you might be picturing something more popular and secular like an egg—an Easter Egg—with its promise of new life; or, again, the Pascal candle, lit at the Easter Eve vigil service which is a very physical reminder of Jesus as the light of the world shining in the darkness bringing hope and enlightenment; or yet again you may be thinking of the font (which is very much like the empty tomb) where in the baptismal waters Christians are born to new life in Christ. You may simply find yourself with the women who ran away frightened or a week later with the disciples who had gathered together in an upper room and were terrified. Whatever image or picture you use requires explanation. The Lenten Group I attended found it very difficult to explain the Easter message in a way that people who were unfamiliar with Christianity could understand. Let us not delude ourselves that the numbers of people unfamiliar with Christianity in our own society grows every day. It is one thing to say Jesus has risen, Hallelujah or to say that he has overcome death or that the Easter faith promises new life, but what do these phrases mean and how do they translate intor21st century society? What is the connection, if there is one, between the resurrection and Diane Pretty who died from Motor Neurone Disease or what has resurrection to do with the world of www. or the net? The challenge to translate the Easter faith into our own society has never been greater.

Easter this year has been somewhat different for me. At the beginning of Lent my father was taken ill and admitted to hospital. He was in hospital for a month before he eventually died, and his funeral was just three weeks ago. When he was first admitted to hospital he was quickly transferred to the Intensive Care Unit. Here he was immediately connected to monitors and various pieces of equipment which provided technical information about his condition. Each patient in the unit is allocated their own nurse on a one-to-one basis and so the care is, as the name indicates, intensive. Patients are only admitted to an Intensive Care Unit if they are seriously ill or indeed close to death. The time my father spent on the unit was exactly three days and then he returned to one of the medical wards. He was quite literally given a new lease of life, albeit it only lasted for another four weeks. Recently, I heard of a doctor who contracted a life-threatening cerebral cyst. He, too, was admitted to the Intensive Care Unit. The cyst was aspirated and three days later he was moved to another ward in the hospital, from where he made a full recovery. It seems that the time required to make this remarkable change in an Intensive Care Unit is often three days. During this time, people literally change from being on the verge of death to independent living.

In the Christian story it was three days that elapsed between Jesus's death and new life. This reference to three days and new life is referred to in other places in the story of the Christian faith. For example, it was on the third day that there was a wedding in Cana of Galilee and Jesus was there with his disciples. There were changes when water was turned into wine and there was the promise of new life which always accompanies a wedding. It is a feature of resurrection and new life that makes the need to change an imperative.

In a very short time—just three days—Jesus effected our redemption and reconciliation with God. This surely is a potent portrayal of the Easter message and the short time—3 days— might just resonate with today's society which IS forever looking for quick results and a rapid response.

Our gospel message for today's world is that death is not an end in itself, but the necessary vehicle of reconciliation and resurrection. Bathe in the glory of Easter and enjoy the festival of resurrection with its promise of glory and new life. Please translate all of this into your daily lives, into your local community, and be ready to share your faith so that others can be transformed by the vibrant message of Easter. Perhaps the empty tomb with the stone rolled away is the way in which you like to picture Easter and its message. If it is, the following poem builds on the image and offers us more insights, as well as an injunction to share Easter with others. It is a poem we can pray.

Roller of Stones

Roller of stones, creator of mists and mystery;
Open me to your life,
Letting your story shine out to the world.
Give me hope, living God, Hope
in my hands to open doors.
Hope in my eyes to see possibilities.
Hope in my heart to live by faith:
For it is hope that rolls away stones.

Julian

There are, in the world, some very special places—places with an atmosphere and nuance all of their own. Often such places are to be found in churches. It is the poet Philip Larkin who refers to them as 'serious places on serious earth'. One such a place is to be found in Norwich near the river. Here in what today is the Red Light District of Norwich is St Julian's Church.

Julian was a 14th Century divine. In the year 1373, when she was thirty years old and suffering from what was considered to be a terminal illness, a woman of Norwich, whose own name is unrecorded, experienced a series of sixteen visions, which revealed aspects of the love of God. Following her recovery, she spent the next twenty years of her life pondering their meaning and recorded her conclusions in what became the first book written by a woman in English, 'Revelations of Divine Love'. At an unknown point in her life, she became an anchoress attached to the Church of St Julian in Norwich, and it was by this name of Julian that she came to be known to later generations. She died around the year 1417.

In the Church of St Julian is the cell where she lived. There is no doubt about it that this is a very special place—a serious place. I have been fortunate enough to have had the privilege to celebrate Holy Communion in the Julian Cell.

There is a stillness, an otherness and a great depth to the atmosphere in this place. This small room on the south side of the church is, I believe, a metaphor for the Church itself. The cell is where Julian lived out her life. It has two windows. One faces the church and through it Julian received Holy Communion. The other faces the outside world. The cell is where she slept and ate, where she said her prayers, where she wrote her divine revelations, where she read her bible, where she meditated and reflected, and where she enjoyed the stillness and the presence of

God. This place was at the centre of her spiritual life, her inner life, her life with God—it was here that she listened to the voice of God and it was here that she spoke to God. It was in this place that she experienced the divine presence and the touch of God upon her life. In her cell she was free to dream, to imagine, to have visions, to let her mind drift beyond the immediate and the visible to the eternal and the hidden. These devout practices nourished and kept alive within her, her Christian faith and the divine spark which was her gift from God.

It is this vision of God, this experience of the divine, this mystery, otherness and holiness that we seek to offer to the world. Our task is to share with people that great truth that Jesus died for the world. This was all part of the inner life of Julian of Norwich which she lived out within the confines of the four walls of her cell.

The window that looks onto the riverside was her link with the outside world and it was here that people would gather for her counsel and advice. They would make their way to the window from the bustling city and the busy riverside port. It would have been a cosmopolitan group of people who came to visit Julian, who came to receive her wisdom, who came to her with their hopes and anxieties, their problems and their joys. It was only 300 years previously that small boats had made their way up the same River Wensum to Pulls Ferry to bring the stone from Caen in France for the new cathedral that was being built by the Normans. Norwich was a very busy port, a place of hustle and bustle where imports from far away countries were stored before onward transportation to the hinterland. It was here that the wool from East Anglia was gathered to be bartered and traded for other goods. Outside it was noisy and bustling, inside it was quiet and still.

Today we mirror the life of Julian. Our outside life is often busy, tense and noisy; at the same time, we seek an inner stillness and tranquillity. Like Julian we are here to serve a bustling world resourced and strengthened by both the grace of God and the assurance of his presence at the centre of inner stillness.

At the heart of the church's ministry is visiting. It is not a particularly popular past-time in the modern world. It is only a tiny percentage of families who, for example, sit down and eat a meal together once a week. Traditional community life has broken down and people today live very privatised lives. Despite this, visiting is nevertheless important and crucial to the life of the Christian community. It is not easy to visit people, especially if you have not met them before. There is always the usual mythology about the Church which has to be addressed— being a very wealthy organisation, vicars only working one day a week, the problems that religion has brought to the world, and a range of misunderstandings and even prejudices. It would be far more difficult for the visitor if they were representing a political party! Never underestimate the value of visiting, especially in an increasingly privatised age. There is nothing as important as human contact and the readiness of one individual to put themselves at the disposal of another. This is the seed bed in which the love of God can grow and flourish. Here are just two examples of the importance of visiting. One became a teaching opportunity, the other a pastoral opportunity.

Two ladies came regularly to the Holy Communion service at their local church but neither actually received communion. The vicar suggested to the churchwarden that they visit them. The churchwarden arranged to see the first lady who explained that she was not allowed to make her communion because she was from the Methodist Church. The churchwarden was able to reassure that the rules had changed and that under new agreements, she would be very welcome to make her communion.

The vicar visited the second lady who was able to receive her communion but preferred to be blessed. She explained that, when the vicar blessed her, he put his hands on her head and this was the only human contact she had from one week to the next.

Visiting is so terribly important, not least because, in the words of the Epistle to the Hebrews, we never know when we might be entertaining angels.

Prayer

Father in Heaven, we long for inner stillness in a busy world. Feed, we pray, our spiritual life with the abundance of your grace and open our eyes to the mystery of your presence. Through the ministrations of others, may the local church community be enriched and people come to know your love and glory, Amen.

Ascension Day

Whether you think that the Feast of the Ascension occurred on Easter day itself or forty days later bringing all the resurrection appearances to a climax does not really affect the importance of this great festival. There are usually six themes associated with the Ascension. The first relies on the tradition of Jesus being lifted up into heaven after he had blessed his disciples on the mountain top. Together they had climbed up to the top of the mountain and then the momentum of moving upwards was to continue when Jesus was lifted up. "Looking up" is important for human beings. We look up to people we admire, we encourage anyone who may be feeling down to cheer up and we look up when we worship God. In the apex of the chapel at Surrey University is a small window known as God's Eye. When people gather there for worship, the window draws their gaze upwards. You could say that upwards is the divine direction. Secondly the Feast of the Ascension marks the final conclusion of Jesus' work. All that needs to be done has been done. Part of the gospel tradition puts the ending of Jesus' work much sooner when, on the cross in St John's gospel, Jesus says "It is finished"; but then, we know that the cross is a throne in the gospel of St John on which Jesus was lifted up into glory. Resurrection and ascension become incorporated into the lifting up of Jesus on the cross.

A third theme running through the celebration of Jesus' ascension is that of Jesus going home. Turn again to St John's gospel and to the opening verses where we are introduced to Jesus as the logos—the word. We read that the word was with God from the beginning and that the word was God. In other words, Jesus' origins were divine and his natural home was with God. Throughout the whole of the gospel John emphasises again and again the special, close relationship between the father and the son. It is a relationship which began in the beginning and is now recaptured when father and son are united. Ascension is truly a homecoming.

In just ten days the feast of Pentecost is celebrated when the spirit of God is given to the church. That same spirit had already been bestowed by Jesus upon his apostles when they gathered in the upper room. It is only when Jesus has completed his work and returned home that the divine power is released to infuse the church with the spirit of God which lived in Jesus. Quite literally we are holding our breath until the day of Pentecost when we celebrate the gift of God's spirit to support and direct our own ministry and mission today. Whether we shall be accused of drinking too much like the first apostles is another matter.

If we turn to St Luke who provides us with the fullest description of the Ascension, we find an interesting phenomenon. Two of his books found their way into the New Testament—the Gospel and the Acts of the Apostles. The movement of Jesus' ministry in St Luke's gospel is from Galilee to Jerusalem where it reaches its crescendo. The Acts of the Apostles begins in Jerusalem and, after the Ascension, when the church has been given the spirit, its mission spreads out from Jerusalem to the world beyond. Jerusalem then is not only a link between the Gospel and the Acts but also a pivotal point where the church's ministry grows out of Jesus' ministry.

Now we turn to the sixth theme associated with the Ascension. Once again it was in St John's gospel that John the Baptist heralded Jesus as the "Lamb of God". This was to connect later with images of the good shepherd and the sheep fold. There is an important and dramatic change in the imagery of the lamb. First Jesus is understood as a sacrificial lamb in the tradition of sacrifice in the Old Testament. Because of his death, resurrection and ascension the lamb changes from being sacrificial to being enthroned. We are offered the image of the lamb enthroned in heaven, not giving glory to God but, as part of the divine Godhead, receiving glory.

In other words, through the Ascension Jesus changes from being our saviour to becoming a focus of our worship. The babe of Bethlehem, the man of Nazareth and the one who gave himself up on the cross takes his rightful place with God the father and God the spirit enthroned in heavenly splendour. It is what John Mason Neale calls "human nature at the father's throne".

Let me end with some words written by George Body. He was Canon Missioner in the Diocese of Durham from 1883 to 1911 and he combined evangelical fervour with Tractarian principles and is a very good example of what is often called "Catholic Evangelicalism". He wrote:-

"The Ascension Day marked a distinct crisis in the worship of God both in heaven and on earth. Until that mysterious morning when Jesus in His assumed Humanity passed within the Veil and took His place within the true Holy of Holies, the "Agnus Dei," the great hymn of Christendom, had never rung through the courts of Heaven; but when the thronging Angels watched the Ascent of the Sacred Humanity of Jesus—and saw its mysterious flight cease only when it was throned on the Right Hand of the Eternal—a new light flashed across their intellects, a new adoration filled their spirits, a new song burst from their lips, a new worship was begun, the worship of Jesus Christ: "Worthy is the Lamb that was slain to receive power, and riches, and wisdom, and strength, and honour, and glory, and blessing!" And as the Ascension of Jesus formed a crisis in the worship of Heaven, so was it also on earth. "They worshipped Him,"—His very withdrawal from among them, His very elevation to the Throne of God, was the development of new relations between the disciples and their Lord. As long as He was on the earth the worship of Him was not the principal feature of their life; but as soon as He was withdrawn from them and seated at God's Right hand in the Heavenly places, the adoration of the Lamb— the worship of Jesus Incarnate, Crucified, Risen, Ascended,

Enthroned—the distinctive worship of the Christian Church—began to be. And a new aspect stood revealed of that holy Eucharist which He had ordained: it was to be the earthly centre of that glorious worship wherewith, in Heaven, in Paradise, and on earth, the Ascended Jesus is ever adored."

Ascension Day is then a very important festival. It is so important that I think it is worth pursuing the reintroduction of the tradition whereby schools are given the day off.

Prayer

We pray that we may embrace the myriad meanings of the Ascension which celebrates the completion of Jesus' work on earth. We pray too that we might look beyond Ascension to the feast of Pentecost and the gift of your spirit which is for each and everyone of us, Amen.

Holy Communion—Then and Now

Last Thursday we celebrated the feast of Corpus Christi. It is the commemoration of the institution and gift of Holy Communion, which traditionally has been celebrated on the Thursday following Trinity Sunday. By C14th, the Feast of Corpus Christi was universally celebrated in the Western Church and in many towns was an occasion for the performance of religious plays, like the Mystery Plays.

In the Church of England up until the last Century the main Sunday morning service was morning prayer. It was only due to the liturgical movement and the development of an initiative called 'Parish and People' that the Catholic Liturgy has been rediscovered with the result that, for the last one hundred years, the Eucharist has been the central act of worship for many people in the Anglican Church. It is easy to understand why the Eucharist appeals to Christian people. It is all embracing and gathers up in thanksgiving the offering of the world and the Church to God to be renewed and reshaped for further service. In the Eucharistic process we, like the bread, are taken and blessed and broken before being recreated by God and sent out, at the end of the service, to minister in the world. The Eucharist is a sacrament instituted by Jesus himself which provides us with spiritual food for our journey of faith. We are refreshed, renewed and re-invigorated by the grace of God which each of us receives through the sacrament. This is all very understandable because the Eucharist gathers together the whole people of God and they are united in the one bread which becomes the one body of Christ—Corpus Christi.

Now things are beginning to change again and the Eucharist is less central than it was, simply because so many people are, as they say, 'unchurched' and have little or no understanding of the Christian faith or what happens in a Church building and, as a consequence the Eucharist has become, in some senses, esoteric. It has become a service for those people who have been initiated into it through baptism and confirmation. We live now in a liturgical world of songs of praise, family services, messy and café church, and fresh expressions. We are being asked to provide a rich menu of worship in order to continue to attract the faithful core and a whole range of other people. In order that the Eucharist continues to have an important place in the worship of the Church, we must ensure that people are taught about it and, at the same time, be ready to make changes so that it becomes more accessible to people. Misunderstandings abound and there is a memorable occasion when I was blessing a young girl who had been brought by her mother to the Communion rail. I saw her patting the top of her head after I had put my hands on her head to bless her. Her mother explained to me afterwards that her daughter thought I had put the communion wafer on her head!

I said earlier that the Holy Communion service had been instituted by Jesus himself at the Last Supper. However, if we look at St John's Gospel, there is no description of the Last Supper. There is no reference to it at all in the account of the last week of Jesus' life. However, if we turn back to chapter six after St John's account of the feeding of the five thousand, we find John's 'version' of the Last Supper. It is this passage which follows Jesus taking the five loaves from the boy blessing them, breaking and distributing them that we find Jesus saying to his Apostles that he is the bread of life. He goes on to tell them that no one who comes to him will ever be hungry. He, Jesus, provides eternal food. Now think about the setting for this last supper, this act of Holy Communion. It was a mass picnic out in the open air—not dissimilar, I guess, from those open air concerts where people take their own food and wine. Some take tables and chairs, candlesticks and flowers, napkins and linen and create an open air dining room. How many open air Eucharists have you attended? The feeding of the five thousand does provide us with another way of thinking about Holy Communion. We do need to think like this, to be much more flexible and more imaginative— ready to take risks and experiment.

Jesus drew a comparison in his Parable of the Wedding Feast to which, you will remember, everyone had been invited. God through Jesus holds open house. Today, we must ensure that the Eucharist is not an act of worship for the privileged and initiated. Like God himself, the Church must hold open house. Only then will we be able to enjoy and experience just how flexible and adaptable the Eucharist can be. It was summed up by the monk, Dom Gregory Dix who wrote ...

"Was ever another command so obeyed? For century after century, spreading slowly to every continent and country and among every race on earth, this action has been done, in every conceivable human circumstance, for every conceivable human need from infancy and before it to extreme old age and after it, from the pinnacle of earthly greatness to the refuge of fugitives in the caves and dens of the earth. Men have found no better thing than this to do for kings at their crowning and for criminals going to the scaffold; for armies in triumph or for a bride and bridegroom in a little country church; for the proclamation of a dogma or for a good crop of wheat; for the wisdom of the Parliament of a mighty nation or for a sick old woman afraid to die; for a schoolboy sitting an examination or for Columbus setting out to discover America; for the famine of whole provinces or for the soul of a dead lover; in thankfulness because my father did not die of pneumonia; for a village headman much tempted to return to fetich because the yams had failed; because the Turk was at the gates of Vienna; for the repentance of Margaret; for the settlement of a strike; for a son for a barren woman; for Captain so-and-so wounded and prisoner of war; while the lions roared in the nearby amphitheatre; on the beach at Dunkirk; while the hiss of scythes in the thick June grass came faintly through the windows of the church; tremulously, by an old monk on the fiftieth anniversary of his vows; furtively, by an exiled bishop who had hewn timber all day in a prison camp near Murmansk; gorgeously, for the canonisation of S. Joan of Arc—one could fill many pages with the reasons why men have done this, and not tell a hundredth part of them. And best of all, week by week and month by month, on a hundred thousand successive Sundays, faithfully, unfailingly, across all the parishes of Christendom, the pastors have done this just to make the plebs sancta Dei—the holy common people of God."

Prayer

Let us pray that we who have been nourished with the food and drink of life eternal, may be a source of nourishment to those whom we seek to serve day by day, Amen.

Symbols of the Spirit

Today is Whitsunday when we celebrate the gift of the Holy Spirit poured out upon the first apostles and subsequently the whole Church.

St Luke's gospel ends with Jesus leaving his apostles to return home to his Father, while they make their way back to Jerusalem to meet and pray. The Acts of the Apostles, St Luke's second volume, begins with the Ascension and moves to Jerusalem where the apostles are to receive the gift of the Holy Spirit.

The journey in St Luke's two volumes moves from Galilee to Jerusalem and then on the first Whitsunday from Jerusalem to the farthest ends of the world.

What a scene it must have been. People were gathered from all over the known world, from places the names of which are a challenge for any reader of the epistle—places like Pamphilia, Cappadocia and Cyrene.

Filled with the Holy Spirit, the apostles were understood by all the people who spoke many different languages. It was a reversal of the Tower of Babel in the book of Genesis which is an account of why there are so many languages spoken in the world.

There are two symbols of the Holy Spirit which are used extensively throughout the Church—they are fire and wind. Both are referred to in today's epistle.

Both fire and wind have positive and negative properties. We make use of fire for warmth and heat; it is used in a variety of processes, e.g. to smelt iron ore in order to make iron girders and produce steel. Like the Holy Spirit, fire generates warmth. Without this, we would become cold and, if the cold persisted unabated, we would die. Fire is also destructive. Often we read of bush fires in Australia and parts of the States particularly, fires in people's houses that often start with the chip pan in the kitchen and fires that burn down schools and other public buildings. Claiming the power of the Holy Spirit can also be destructive. Think for a moment of those Christian sects which have claimed the Holy Spirit as their own. They then speak as though it is the Holy Spirit at work within them, but their extravagant and bizarre utterings can hurt and destroy people. In some of these sects, such rantings have led to mass suicide. Like fire, the Holy Spirit has to be treated with respect and held in awe. Like any power for good the Holy Spirit can be manipulated and used by people with misguided and sometimes divisive intent to bring about harm and damage. Every time I wear this red chasuable I am reminded of the symbol of fire for the Holy Spirit because of the sheet of flame embroidered on the front of the vestment.

There was a sound like that of a rushing mighty wind; the other symbol for the spirit of God is wind. You will recall that, in the first verses of the book of Genesis, we are told of the spirit of God breathing over the waters of creation to infuse it with life and vigour. This spirit is the breath of God and, to this day in Greek Orthodox rites of baptism, the Bishop will breathe over the baptismal waters to indicate that it is here that Christian people begin a new life. We know from our own experience how the rush of air into a baby's lungs signals a new way of living for the newborn baby. Up until this time the baby has lived in a very different way inside its mother. It has lived a water life like a fish, but then its lungs fill with air and it begins to live a different life and breathe of its own accord. The very word that is translated from the New Testament for spirit means air or wind and gives us words in the English language like pneumonia and pneumatic.

Without the wind, you cannot fly a kite, sail a boat or use a weather vane. Historically, people have relied upon the wind to fill the sails of the great ships that used to ply the oceans. We need the Holy Spirit to blow us along our pilgrim way—if you will, to fill our spiritual sails and continually to breathe into us the life of God himself.

Wind, like fire, can also be destructive. It can wreck huge buildings, bring down trees and whip up the waters of the sea. We only have to think of the havoc and destruction that was caused by the wind, particularly in the south of England, in the late 80s and more recently tsunamis. Many of the trees have not been replaced and the countryside has changed as a result . The irony is that trees are often planted as protection against the wind and to provide wind breaks. Once again, we are reminded very forcibly of the need to approach the Holy Spirit of God with care and understanding, to take nothing for granted and be aware of just how easily people can use the Holy Spirit to manipulate others to their own ends.

We have, then, these two symbols of fire and wind and my chasuable reminds me of the fire of the Holy Spirit of God and my bicycle pump of the Spirit as wind or air. May each and every one of you be filled with the Spirit of God this Pentecost.

Prayer

Thank you for the gift of your Holy Spirit which we celebrate at Pentecost each year. May we and the whole church be filled with the power of your Spirit to encourage us to share your love and promises for the world. We pray that the peace of your Spirit may infuse the world and its leaders to establish lasting peace in every generation, Amen.

Fatherhood

Today's Gospel reading is very well known to all of us. Amongst other things, it is one of a number of bible readings used at funerals because of its emphasis on looking forward into the heavenly realms where there are many rooms in God's house. This is very reassuring because there is likely to be as much variety from one person to another in heaven as there is on earth. There have been many occasions when I have used this idea of different rooms for different people at funeral services; so, for example, I might identify the person who has died with the family room or the game's room.

In the reading we are invited to listen to the conversation that is taking place between Jesus and his friends. Jesus encourages his disciples not to be anxious or troubled but to believe in God and in him. He talks about the future, assuring them that there is a place for them and that he will be with them. Doubting Thomas declares that he was never very good at geography and does not know the way. Jesus responds with some of the most important words attributed to him—'I am the way, and the truth, and the life. No one comes to the Father except by me'. These words are important for three reasons.

1.   He repeats the theme that is developed throughout St John's Gospel that he and the Father are one. By identifying Jesus' true nature we are able to identify God. Oneness is a central theme to the gospel narrative and unique to this gospel.

2.   Jesus uses the phrase 'I am' not once but seven times in the fourth gospel. He says 'I am the true vine, I am the good shepherd, I am the bread of life, and I am the way'. These words 'I am' are important because in the Old Testament it is the name of God himself (I am what I am)

and Jesus' hearers will have known this and realised that Jesus identified himself with God or, as he expresses it in the St John's Gospel, 'The Father and I are one'. It was this claim that led to his death and one which many did not understand. Clergy come across, sadly, an increasing number of people who do not understand who Jesus is. They know from the many funerals that they conduct that today, if people are to join in the words of the Lord's Prayer, the words need to be printed because many people do not know the words by heart.

3.   Jesus says that he is the way and that no one comes to the Father except by him. It is these words that I would like to concentrate on particularly for a moment.

'No one comes to the Father except by me'—these words have been consistently used, I believe mistakenly, to support and ratify the contention that salvation is possible only through Jesus. People who support this view which clearly is exclusive and allows no room for any other way of approaching God be it Jewish, Islam, Hindu, or Sikh, appeal to this text to justify their understanding of salvation. The words 'I am the way' are quoted liberally to establish a single route to God and salvation. Not only is it a fundamentalist position but also excludes the other great world religions. This is a serious matter particularly in our own multi-cultural and multi-faith society and in a society which historically has been renowned for its tolerance and openess.

Tolerance is a political issue in relation to migrant workers and asylum seekers and in some quarters there seems to be a loss of memory. This country is part of the wider European federation and already there are one million British people with properties in Spain and a half million with properties in France. I am increasingly concerned to discover that the BNP is putting up candidates in towns here in Lincolnshire. Openness and tolerance are not values associated with this particular organization nor is it sensitive to the needs of a variety of groups of people from other countries. Running through the pages of the Old Testament and central to the Christian Gospel is the imperative to welcome the stranger and the foreigner. Such a welcome is a mark of a community of faith and of a civilized society. The task of every Christian person is to speak out on behalf of those whom we find on the margins of society, whom others have rejected and for whom Jesus died.

Let us then return to the words of Jesus—'No one comes to the Father except by me'. The words and the detail are important. Jesus did not say in the Fourth Gospel 'no one comes to God except by me' but 'no one comes to the Father ....'. What Jesus is explaining to his disciples and, therefore, to you and me is not an exclusive route to God which is only possible through him, Jesus, but the possibility of a relationship with God as a father. It is God's fatherhood which is paramount and which is emphasized again and again throughout the whole of St John's Gospel. The prayer most frequently found on Christian lips is the Lord's Prayer which begins with the words 'Our Father'. Immediately we are addressing God as father and just as he was the father of our Lord Jesus Christ, so he is our Heavenly Father. This is what is unique to the Christian faith. This, if you like, is our claim to exclusivity. Ours is the one faith whose God walked this earth and who, through the drama of the cross and resurrection, offers us salvation. Here, in the person of Jesus, is the vehicle for us to approach the Heavenly Father and enter the presence of God where we can experience and enjoy the love of an Eternal Father. It is a truth that needs to be heard more than ever in contemporary society and is incumbent upon the church to proclaim.

Prayer

Be with us in our struggle to overcome prejudice, bigotry and fundamentalism and, good Lord, ensure that there are always many ways to approach you and that you offer many rooms within your heavenly house to provide comfort and refuge for those who seek your presence, Amen.

The Trinity

At the turn of the first Millennium the Church in the east and the Church in the west divided and, sad to say, they remain divided to this day. They divided over political, ecclesiastical and theological differences—the theological disagreement was about a single Latin word—filioque. In English it means 'and the son'. The words are from the Nicene Creed which is said at each holy communion service. The original creed was laid down at the Council of Nicaea in 325 from which it takes its name. The filioque clause was introduced at the Council of Toledo in 589. The Creed, as we say it today, states that the Holy Spirit proceeds from the Father and the Son and these words have been said in the western Church over many centuries.

However, at the turn of the first Millennium the Church in the east argued against the incorporation of the words 'and the Son' and wished only for the Holy Spirit to proceed from the Father which led to the Great Schism in 1054.

It is probably easier to explain what I mean by looking at the following two diagrams. I ought to say at the outset that this is not a lesson in geometry nor is it about equilateral triangles! Here then are the diagrams:

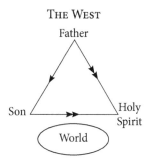

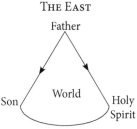

Here the Holy Spirit proceeds from the Father and the Son.

Here the Holy Spirit proceeds only from the Father and not the Son. This provides a concept of the Trinity where God is open to the World and the World is incorporated into the Godhead.

In the Western church, as the diagrams indicate the Godhead is separate from the World which gives rise to expresions like 'God is in his heaven and all is well with the world'. Such a theology nurtures Deism which is not a feature of the christian faith and division between God and the world he created.

The theology of the Holy Trinity which underpins the Orthodox faith of the east centering on Byzantium, envisages a close relationship between God and the world, so much so that the two are irrevocably linked. Quite simply it means that the world enters the Godhead and this has implications for the way in which the Church in the east arranges its buildings and its liturgy. Because the church is the House of God, then stepping into the church means stepping into Heaven and so the churches of the east—Russian and Greek Orthodox—have richly decorated interiors where the use of icons predominate. For Christians of this persuasion, when they hear the words 'therefore with angels and archangels and with the whole of company of Heaven we laud and magnify thy glorious name evermore praising Thee and saying Holy, Holy, Holy...', quite literally they believe that at this point Heaven and Earth are one. The interior of the church building is far more important than the exterior and the liturgy needs to be such that people are given the experience that they are part of the heavenly host singing with angels and archangels. I think it is clear from what I have said that I favour the Orthodox creed without Filioque simply because it allows God to embrace the world and the whole of creation where everyone has a part to play. More importantly is what you think!

John the Baptist

(St John Chapter 1 verses 6 and 7)
'There was a man sent from God whose name was John. He came as a witness to testify to the light, so that all might belive through him.'

One of the greatest names of the industrial revolution was Isambard Kingdom Brunel. He is one of my favourite people not just because I like pronouncing his name but also because, as well as being an internationally acclaimed engineer, he was a bridge builder.

I first became aware of the proliferation of iron bridges when I began my ministry as a curate in the West Midlands. One of Brunel's earliest bridges to be built was the suspension bridge over the River Avon at Clifton and another is the old Hungerford Bridge in London. As well as being a designer of iron steamships and the engineer for the Great Western Railway— God's Wonderful Railway, the last great bridge he built was the Royal Albert at Saltash over the Tamar. This bridge linked Devon with Cornwall. People were very doubtful of Brunel's ability to bridge such a wide stretch of water. Brunel began by sinking two substantial pillars in the river and sending to Glasgow and Newcastle for iron girders long enough to reach the brick pillars. He is supposed to have said "If you give me the lifting force, I can do anything". These words echo other words familiar to us "If you ask anything in my name ...."

All this talk about Isambard Kingdom Brunel is because on June 24 we celebrate that great biblical figure, John the Baptist. Brunel was a bridge builder and so, too, was John the Baptist. In the secular world Brunel built bridges which enabled people to travel and communicate. This too is an activity central to the mission of the Church. For the Church has the task of building bridges between the scared and the secular in order to help people travel, to facilitate communication and to inspire the whole idea of pilgrimage. John the Baptist was not only a bridge builder but was also a bridge himself because he linked the Old Testament and the New. He was the fulcrum, as it were, between the Jewish religion and the Christian faith. Essentially, he was a theological bridge builder and this is because, having looked forward for so long to the coming of the Messiah, it was John the Baptist who identified Jesus and heralded him as the Lamb of God.

Another person who has this bridge building responsibility is the Pope. He is called Pontifex Maximus and the word 'Pontifex' means bridge maker and so the Pope is called to be the master bridge maker. This papal responsibility can be understood in a number of different ways. For example, the Pope is the person to build bridges throughout the worldwide Roman Catholic Church. He might also be seen as one who seeks to build bridges with other parts of the Church and to create bridges between the Church and the world. Not sovery long ago, with so many other people we prayed for Cardinal Basil Hume that he may rest in peace, grow in love and rise in glory. Cardinal Hume in a very humble and holy way sought to build bridges and overcome division.

Without a willingness to look beyond itself and establish bridgeheads, the Church will become introspective. Unless the Church is open to the world, it will die—hardly the mission Jesus had in mind when he sent out 72 of his followers to build bridges, or when he gave his great exhortation at the end of St

Matthew's gospel "Go forth and baptise people everywhere in the name of the Father and of the Son and of the Holy Spirit".

John the Baptist was not only a bridge builder and a means of linking the Old and the New Testament, his more familiar title is that of 'Forerunner'. Another reason why John the Baptist means a great deal to me is because two of the churches where I have worked have been dedicated to him. One was near Norwich, the other in Kidderminster where the parish magazine was called the Forerunner. One of the senior clergy in the Diocese told me recently that John the Baptist was the first Archdeacon! This immediately set me thinking because I began to wonder what he had in mind. Did he think, for example, that Archdeacons lived on locusts and honey or that they needed a haircut or, indeed, a thoroughly good bath? What he had in mind, I am sure, was the link with John the Baptist as a forerunner. He prepared the way. He was the man sent from God, whose name was John. He came to bear witness to the Light. As the Collect for the day says ... 'He was wonderfully born to fulfil your purpose by preparing the way for the advent of your Son' and it goes on ... 'Lead us to repent according to his preaching and after his example constantly to speak the truth, boldly rebuke vice, and patiently suffer for the truth's sake ... ' His was a ministry of preparation and it involved speaking out boldly in order to clear the way for the one that was to follow. Perhaps, after all, this is one role for an Archdeacon—to be out in front trying to prepare the way. It was my predecessor who used to say that the Archdeacon entered the church by the back door and the Bishop by the front. One of the features of the Baptist's ministry is the introduction of Jesus to the people of Israel. As Jesus increases in stature and becomes known by more and more people, so John decreases and fades into the background. This is the role of any pioneer or forerunner. The idea of pioneer evokes pictures of the wild west, of covered wagons crossing the prairies.

It is much easier to be a settler, the other group in the American west, than a pioneer. Pioneers in the church today are contemporary John the Baptists—people who prepare the way, constantly speak the truth and boldly rebuke vice. Pioneers work on the frontiers of society often with people others ignore, discard or reject—the very people whom Jesus made a priority in his ministry—sinners, lepers, tax gathers, and Samaritans. The job of Christians today is to seek out the equivalent groups and offer them support, care and love. Once the ministry is established and growing, it is time then to move on, to decrease and blend into the background.

How appropriate it is then when, during a service, there is a baptism. The Baptist used the River Jordan, we tend not to use a river but a font in which water is poured and blessed and then the Christian sign is placed on the candidate's forehead. It is invisible but permanent, the Cross, the sign of Christ, marked by the priest. It is invisible but permanent, the Cross, the sign of Christ, marked by the priest. From this moment a new life begins—a pioneer life preparing the way with others in the Church.

Here is a copy of a hymn especially written to celebrate John the Baptist and the last verse reads as follows :

John the Baptist, saint and prisoner,
Murdered at Salome 's whim,
Herald of the Gospel message
You inspire our festal hymn.
John the Baptist, preacher, prophet,
We salute you and proclaim
You the bridge between two faiths.
Today we celebrate your name.

Prayer

Almighty God, by whose providence your servant John the Baptist was wonderfully born, and sent to prepare the way of your Son our Saviour

By the preaching of repentance: lead us to repent according to his preaching and, after his example, constantly to speak the truth, boldly rebuke vice and patiently suffer for the truth's sake, Amen.

Deacons

'Therefore, friends, select from among yourselves seven men
of good standing, full of the spirit and of wisdom, whom we
may appoint to this task—to wait at table'
(Acts 6 vs.3)

In this morning's service the Bishop of Repton will ordain ten
deacons—seven women and three men. This is both a formal
and legal service and already the candidates have taken their
oaths before the Bishop and his legal officer, the Registrar. Now
they are to be ordained by the Bishop and admitted to the office
of a deacon in the church of God.

Our prayer today for each of the candidates is that they will be
filled with the spirit of God. We pray that through the grace of
God they will be equipped to undertake their work as deacons
in the church of God.

Services like this one only happen two or three times a year
and so they are very special occasions, of course, for the deacons,
their families and friends but also for the wider church. Today is
the first time that they are able to wear a clerical collar. Welcome
to the club!

Over the last four days we have been living, praying and
working together and have been looking particularly at the life
and work of both the deacon and the priest. The candidates have
spent not only the last few days but many months and years
preparing for this moment. Today is then very special because it
is the climax of years of hard work and preparation

Like any organization the church is changing rapidly and so
too is the work of the clergy. Increasingly clergy work with a
range of people some of whom are paid but the majority are
volunteers. Increasingly the church will be served by volunteers
with volunteers for volunteers. Of our twenty candidates this

weekend ten are stipended or paid and ten are non stipendiary.

So you are to be deacons and the word has two meanings—serving and waiting. There are innumerable ways in which people serve the needs of others. Every year a noble peer from the House of Lords travels North to a Franciscan Friary where she spends a fortnight cleaning the bathrooms and corridors. It is good for the soul, she says Every week volunteers from the WRVS serve tea and coffee in the local hospital. Every day on the streets of Calcutta sisters from Mother Theresa's order gather up the destitute and dying and take them to their house to care for them. In the text from the Acts of the Apostles we heard how seven men were chosen to serve at the tables. After the Bishop has ordained you, your stole will be placed over your left shoulder and you will wear it like this until you are ordained as a priest. It is much very like a waiter who puts his dish cloth over his arm or shoulder. It is a reminder of the ministry of a deacon, a ministry of service. A deacon is a waiter and so it follows that an Archdeacon is then a head waiter.

Jesus expressed his service to his Apostles in a different way. He washed their feet which amazed them because it broke all the usual conventions. Later in today's service the Bishop will be faithful to this tradition and wash your feet, reminding all of us of his ministry of service.

The second meaning of the word deacon is waiting. In the U.K. we are renowned for the orderly way in which we queue and the infinite patience we show, especially at places like airports. Waiting is second nature to us. First as people in Holy Orders we are called to wait upon God. This is a daily exercise and the waiting begins when we wake up and say our prayers. Do not wait to say your prayers, otherwise you will find that you quickly run out of time and the prayers are left unsaid. It is when we are praying and spending time quietly, often early in the day that we can wait upon God and discern His will for us. Prayer is our conversation with God which involves both listening as well as speaking.

During the next twelve months you will also be waiting to become priests and learning more about the ministry of the priest.

Lastly waiting has a vital role to play in our pastoral ministry, especially when you have to wait for a person to reach a point where they feel safe enough to unburden themselves to you. Here is the heart of the sacred ministry when you help a person who is anxious or distressed to feel secure and supported by the love of God and His divine embrace. It is a huge responsibility and a great privilege.

When you leave the cathedral, you will go into the world a changed person. Your badge of office is your clerical collar. You may sometimes forget that you are wearing it, others will not. The world today is not an easy place for a person wearing a clerical collar. In the West the climate is aggressively secular where many want to see the demise of the church. It is multi cultural and multi faith. A multi faith society places a responsibility upon you to be clear about your own beliefs. Rest assured you will be asked what you believe and people will expect answers.

People do not usually distinguish between a deacon and a priest and a bishop and an archdeacon. We are all called 'vicar'. The harvest is great, the labourers are few and there is much to be done. Go from here and through the grace of God exercise your ministry of service and waiting. We, in turn, will all pray for you today and every 4th of July hereafter, Amen.

Prayer

May all deacons in the church be true and effective servants in the ministry of your gospel. May they also, we pray, learn to wait upon you and your word and those they are called to serve.

Give them courage as they exercise their ministry at times when they confront indifference, bigotry and the challenges of secularism, Amen.

Priests

"You shall be called priests of the Lord and be named ministers of our God." (Isaiah 61 verse 6a)

In this morning's service the Bishop will ordain seven priests. This is both a formal and legal service and already the candidates have taken their oaths before the Bishop and his legal officer, the Registrar. Now they are to be ordained by the Bishop and admitted to the office of a priest.

Perhaps you have never been to an Ordination service before. Perhaps you have not been to Lincoln Cathedral before. Perhaps our ceremonies seem somewhat strange and unfamiliar. As the procession made its way along the nave you may well have played spot the Dean, spot the Archdeacon and spot the Bishop. Spotting the Bishop is easy because he is the only one who wears a hat. The shape of the hat is important because it represents flames and flames are a symbol of the Holy Spirit. Our prayer today for each of the priests is that they will be filled with the spirit of God. We pray that through the grace of God they will be equipped to undertake their work as priests in the church of God.

Services like this one only happen two or three times a year and so they are very special occasions, of course, for the priests, their families and friends but also for the wider church. A year ago each of them was ordained as a deacon which is the first time that they were invited to wear a clerical collar.

Over the last three days we have been living, praying and working together and have been looking particularly at the life and work of the priest. The candidates have spent not only the last few days but many months and years preparing for this moment. Today is then very special because it is the climax of years of hard work and preparation

Like any organization the church is changing rapidly and so too is the work of a vicar. Increasingly vicars work with a range of people some of whom are paid but the majority are volunteers. However much the role may be changing, the vicar is first and foremost a pastor and a priest.

The pastoral work involves visiting the sick in hospital, in residential homes and in the privacy of a person's own home. Each of you will spend time with the anxious and confused, with people who approach you with particular problems, with people who want you to pray for them (and they make the assumption that your prayers are better than theirs), and with people who are dying. When you sit with a dying person you may well hold their hand, say very little but pray a great deal. As a pastor you will be giving people time and, for some of them, they will never have experienced this before—a person making them the focus of attention, valuing them and treating them with dignity and with kindness. You will also meet people at times of joy and celebration when babies are born, when couples commit themselves to one another in marriage, when you accompany candidates for confirmation whom you have prepared over the months before, and when people turn to you to rededicate their lives and renew promises. Being a pastor is not optional because it feeds your prayer life and is a rich resource for your sacramental ministry.

As well as being a pastor which you have already experienced during your year as a deacon, you are called to be a priest. The focus of the priesthood is found essentially in the administration of the sacraments.

In our tradition Bishops ordain and confirm, but we administer the other five sacraments. As well as baptism, marriage and Holy Communion, there is absolution and anointing. These last two are very personal and often very private. Remember Jesus' words about the sins we loose and the sins we retain. Retaining someone's sin is an awesome responsibility. In our post modern age consolation, confession and absolution are sought among a range of people from the psychiatrist to the fortune teller.

Nevertheless, people will turn to you and to the church and we need to be ready to offer them the church's sacraments.

On life's stage the priest occupies more than one place. Much of the priestly ministry is spent on the edges of society where we find the people to whom Jesus ministered himself. Here we find the broken and rejected, the desperate and the needy, the unloved and the unlovely. These are the people that others have rejected and banished to the outer fringes of society—a society which reinforces the obsessional self centredness of the current age without any understanding of the all embracing love of God that knows no boundaries and values everyone.

At other times we find ourselves at the centre of the stage, most especially when we celebrate Holy Communion—the Eucharist.

The sacrament of Holy Communion speaks to us in a particular way because it is here that we meet Jesus in all his fullness. The gospel evidence for this is to be found in the village of Emmaus. Outside the retreat house at Southwell is a sculpture entitled "The Road to Emmaus". It is beautifully crafted and depicts 3 scenes. The first is of two people making their way back to the village of Emmaus. The second shows them being joined by a third person and in the last scene they are all seated around a table and the visitor is taking the bread on the table, giving thanks, breaking it and distributing it. As soon as this happened, their eyes were opened and they recognised the stranger. It was the risen Christ.

The Eucharist signals a change in Jesus between this world and eternity. Jesus the sacrificial lamb becomes Jesus the enthroned lamb and therefore a focus of worship. At the Last Supper, Jesus is at pains to stress how the master must become the servant; and all his disciples must learn to be both host and guest in their relationships and expression of courtesy and service towards each other.

Yes, the Eucharist is a foretaste of the heavenly banquet; it is also the place where we come to be broken and renewed and given the grace of God. Only then can we undertake our ministry of service to those who are broken in the world. This will demand that we recognise Jesus in the other person. The image of recognition is important. Jesus puts this very succinctly: "The last shall be first and the first last" recognising others as equals and recognising their needs directly affects who we ultimately are before God.

The Eucharist is the one act of Christian worship which brings together God's word, God's people, God's ministers, and God's food. It is here that we are fed with the food of eternity. In Holy Communion bread is taken, blessed, broken, and distributed. To be the Body of Christ in the world, we too have to be ready to be taken, blessed, broken, and shared. It is our privilege and our obligation at Holy Communion to take the things of this world—bread and wine–and, in placing them on the altar table, to continue the story of remembering and to join our hands with those of Jesus as we engage in the consecration of God's food. Here we join with the angels and archangels and the whole company of Heaven to share the food of eternity.

Mark, David, Peter, Pamela, Jane, Diana, and Graham, it is a huge responsibility to be a pastor and a priest and it is the best thing in the world.

I am particularly grateful to the Bishop for the opportunity to conduct the ordination retreat and preach in the cathedral today because tomorrow I retire. What better way could I have of finishing my ministry on the day each of you begin your work as priests. We pray for you today and we shall remember you on every 29th day of June hereafter.

Prayer

Bless, we pray, all priests and fill them with your grace and the power and comfort of the Holy Spirit. Be with each priest in their pastoral and sacramental ministries; may they ever be servants to those in their care and be full of loving kindness and confidence to preach, interpret and translate the gospel into action, Amen.

St Thomas

Today, St Thomas' day, in the revised calendar is the anniversary of my ordination to the priesthood (47 years ago!). It is an important day for any priest and it really doesn't matter whether you are a Rural Dean, an Archdeacon, a Bishop or even an Archbishop. At heart all are priests, as I used to remind some Bishops with whom I worked . In fact, my doctrine tutor used to remind us that in Heaven there are no Bishops only priests, because the one Bishop—Jesus himself from whom everything originates—is there in person.

In the old Lectionary 21 December was celebrated as St Thomas' day and so naturally he has a special place in my heart. You will remember that he was Thomas the doubter. He even doubted Jesus' resurrection until, he said, he could place his fingers where the nails had been, he would *not* believe. Thomas represents a particular tradition and, in a way, St Paul represents a very different tradition which was summed up for us in the Epistle. St Paul works out the scheme of salvation, has it all sewn up and there is an air of assurance and certainty about it. Such a tradition is very much alive in the church today. Such certainty can easily lead to fundamentalism which combines certainty without question and faith without doubt.

Fundamentalism is not peculiar to Christianity. You only have to think of the Jehovah's Witness who arrives on your doorstep locked into their own brand of fundamentalism and obsessional thinking. It was a Bishop of Grimsby, no less, who, when confronted with a Jehovah's Witness, asked who they were and the person replied, "Jehovah's Witness" and he said, "No you are not. I am." and then he shut the door. No good really comes from fundamentalism because it breeds arrogance and eventually dictatorship and that is exactly what is happening with *IS*.

The Thomist approach is not slightly different, but very

different. Our faith grows and develops simply because we are prepared to ask questions and have doubts—if you understand the inheritance of the faith as something that is dynamic, changing and responding as the Gospel meets the world it seeks to serve. This is the tradition of that great Bishop of Durham, David Jenkins, who insisted against great opposition that first we must make sure that we ask questions and secondly that we ask the right questions. His ministry in Durham actually resulted in Durham miners talking in the pubs about the resurrection and cramming into Durham Cathedral on Easter when, by tradition, the diocesan bishop preaches and Bishop Jenkins was no exception. In a similar way, a bishop of Grantham with whom I worked persuaded Fenland farmers that there is life beyond death.

What this really all amounts to is how we think about God. Increasingly I believe in a God who is prepared to take risks. I believe in a God who is open and approachable. He is not a God who has everything neatly compartmentalised and packaged. He is also She and a God beyond gender who calls us to live a life of love, to take risks, to ask questions, to humanise the inhuman, even to turn the world upside down as Jesus did.

So we may ask where did Jesus learn his faith? The answer is the one which is the similar for thousands of children. First he learned about the world and God from his parents. It seems to me that Mary responded to God in a lively and decisive way. Read again the Magnificat, Mary's song, and there are the central truths of the Gospel—a sense of wonder in the presence of God, a recognition of the hope of salvation, a realisation of the part she was to play in the salvation of humanity, the establishment of God's Kingdom on earth where goodness and justice reign, and there is a care for the poor and the hungry. Mary responded in faith to the voice of God. Hers was a faith in which she placed her hope in God. There were no certainties but rather the beginning of a pilgrimage which was to take her from the stable in Bethlehem to her home behind the carpenter's shop in Nazareth, into the Galilean countryside to listen to her Son speaking with authority, telling stories in parables and unfolding truths about God, a journey which was to take her from Nazareth and Galilee to Jerusalem where her Son was arrested, tried and executed. Her journey did not stop here, but centred on an upper room where once again she was in the presence of her Son, a journey which ended with her being cared for by one of his own followers—a small band of people who seemed confident and filled with hope and ready to conquer the world. None of this could she have foreseen when she first became aware that she was going to have a child who would be the Son of God.

It is the faith of Mary and the faith of Thomas and the faith of David Jenkins, that surely is the faith that we need today. It is a faith of hope, a faith which encourages us to take risks and not look back, a faith which urges us forward on our pilgrimage, and a faith which enables us to live in the loving embrace of God. It is a faith which can uphold the vision of peace so wonderfully expressed by the prophet Isaiah….

"The wolf shall live with the lamb, the leopard shall lie down with the kid, the calf and the lion and the fatling together, and a little child shall lead them. The cow and the bear shall graze, their young shall lie down together; and the lion shall eat straw like the ox. The nursing child shall play over the hole of the asp, and the weaned child shall put its hand on the adder's den. They will not hurt or destroy on all my holy mountain; for the earth shall be full of the glory of God until the waters fill the sea."

Seeing is Believing

One of the extra responsibilities I had as an Archdeacon was to train new Archdeacons. There are 121 altogether in the Church of England. At one of the last training conferences other than eight Archdeacons in England, there was also the Archdeacon of the Isle of Man, Camarthen, Gibraltar, Switzerland and North West Europe. This was the third such conference in which I had been involved and it was certainly the most varied. There are seven Archdeacons altogether in Europe, one of whom was also the Dean of the cathedral in Gibraltar; for three of them to have been new appointments must be some sort of record. I was intrigued to discover that the Archdeacon for Eastern Europe covers an area from Vienna to Vladivostok—even larger than the Archdeaconry of Lincoln!

One of the guest speakers was the Chancellor of the diocese of Chelmsford who, as you may imagine, was responsible for a session on Faculties and the Diocesan Advisory Committee. At one stage, he divided the group into two. One of the smaller groups was asked to provide reasons why photographs might be included on memorials in churchyards and the other to provide reasons why they should not. I joined the group which was asked to provide reasons why the Regulations might be changed to allow photographs and there were five in all. The first was that the technology is now available to enable this to happen and secondly there may well be very good pastoral reasons which would be helpful and supportive of people during a time of bereavement. The third reason was that the practice already happens in the Church in Wales and fourthly England is now a multi-racial society and many of the Eastern European countries and certainly Italy include photographs as standard practice. The last reason given was to do with the post-modern age in which we all live. The point was made that it is a very visual age with the emphasis being more on what we see than on what we hear or read. Photographs naturally lend themselves to this sort of culture.

I want to concentrate on this emphasis on the visual for a moment in relation to today's Gospel. The story is the familiar account of the two Disciples making their way from Jerusalem to Emmaus when they are joined by a third party. The story is really about a shift from not seeing and not believing to seeing and then believing. There is another post-resurrection experience of Jesus which deals with the same phenomenon. Two weeks after Easter, we find the Apostles gathered together and among them is Thomas who featured prominently in this morning's gospel. He is not prepared to believe what the others are telling him about Jesus' resurrection. He wants to see for himself before he is ready to believe and, you will remember, Jesus shows him the marks of the nails and his side which had been pierced by the soldier's lance. Thomas' unbelief turns to belief once he has the visual evidence in front of him.

So much of what we deal with in the Christian faith is not immediately visible. Values like justice and peace and virtues like faith and love and attributes like holiness and mystery are difficult to put into visual form. We can talk about them, we can read about them and we can experience them but often it is difficult to see them. However, there are other aspects of the Christian life which are visible. These are the Sacraments and chief among them is the Sacrament of Holy Communion. Holy Communion has been celebrated in a whole variety of settings and at the house in Emmaus, it was on the dining room table. Once the stranger who had accompanied the two Disciples took the bread and blessed it, broke it and distributed it, then their eyes were opened. At this very particular point they saw and they believed and everything that had happened and been said on the journey from Jerusalem to Emmaus fell into place. For Thomas, the evidence was the marks of the crucifixion. For the two Disciples on their way to Emmaus, the evidence was the blessed and broken bread. We still have that evidence available to us today every time we come to Holy Communion. We too can move from not seeing and not believing to seeing and believing. However, never forget the words of Jesus himself who reminded Thomas that those who have not seen and yet believe are blessed.

The ending of the story about Emmaus is very important. As soon as the two Disciples see and believe, even though it is late at night, they leave the house and return to Jerusalem to share their experience with the other Apostles. They engaged in what today we would call the mission activity of the Church. Once we have shared the bread which has been taken and blessed and broken, we too leave in order to take our part in the mission of the Church. At the end of every Communion Service I use a prayer I wrote some years ago. I hope it reflects both the ministry and the mission of the church. The words are …..

We thank you, Lord, for nourishing us
with the food and drink of life eternal.
We pray that we may be a source of nourishment
to those whm we seek to serve day by day, Amen.

Pilgrimage Routes

At the time St Hugh was Bishop of Lincoln, pilgrimage was at its height. Across Europe there were tens of thousands of pilgrims on the move. The three great centres were Jerusalem and particularly the Holy Sepulchre, St Peter's in Rome, and Santiago De Compostella in Galicia in north western Spain. Later on in England pilgrims first and foremost made their way to Canterbury to the shrine of Thomas a Becket but running a very close second was the shrine of St Hugh in Lincoln. Because of the Crusader Wars it became increasingly difficult to reach Jerusalem and so Santiago became a pilgrimage attraction. Additionally Christians in northern Spain sought support from their neighbours and allies to help resist the threat of Muslim insurgents from the south.

The discovery of the tomb of St James came almost a century after the Muslims had invaded and occupied almost the whole of the Iberian peninsular; Galicia was in the front line in the battle against them. Alfonso II, King of Asturias and Galicia, needed support from elsewhere in Europe, as did the rulers of the other tiny kingdoms bordering Galicia in northern Spain and so they encouraged pilgrimage and the development of the shrine of

Sant-Iago (St James). It is said that Theodomir and a local hermit, Pelagius, were led by a star to a field in which they found a tomb containing three burial chambers. The two men had no doubt that one of them contained the remains of St James. The belief was that James had been charged by Jesus himself with converting the people of the Iberian Peninsula.

The name Compostella is often said to be a corruption of Campus Stellae or 'field of the star' and so refers to the way in which the tomb had been found. An alternative explanation is that it derived from the Latin word for a cemetery. However, all of this is part of the legend and the belief that St James was buried at

Compostella. This is important because he was the only apostle to be buried in western Europe outside Rome. Within 50 years the pilgrimage route to Santiago de Compostella became one of the most important in the Christian world and every twenty-fifth day of July his festival is celebrated. When it is a holy year the pilgrims' door in the Cathedral near the shrine is opened.

Four pilgrim routes crossed France from Italy, Germany and the Netherlands. Pilgrims from other countries further north and east joined the routes at places like Vezelay and Le Puy. Soon great pilgrimage churches sprang up along these routes, built in the architectural style of the 11th and 12th centuries— Romanesque. Some of the churches were monolithic and very grand like St Sernin in Toulouse, others smaller and beautiful like St Faith at Conques. The whole enterprise was given an added impetus and dimension by the great Benedictine monastic order—the hub of which was at Cluny in Burgundy.

The four pilgrimage routes were described in a remarkable document compiled in the 1130s. It was really an early guidebook and gave practical information on some of the hazards pilgrims would meet, the nature of the regions through which they would travel, the people who inhabited them, and the important shrines en route, including a detailed description of the cathedral in Santiago as it was at that time. The traditional pilgrim's equipment consisted of a broad-brimmed hat, a long cloak, a small pouch or scrip for some food and personal belongings, a gourd or something similar to carry water, sandals and a long staff tipped by an iron ferrule to serve both as a walking stick and as a weapon in case of attack. It was only after they reached Santiago that pilgrims were entitled to wear the shell which was the symbol of the pilgrim.

On the southern route the pilgrim would have passed through St Giles in Provence and seen its imposing western façade. Giles' care for the wounded and those crippled by disease resulted in his becoming the patron saint of such people, particularly of those with leprosy. Leprosy sufferers were not permitted to enter towns and cities and therefore often congregated on the outskirts, where churches built to meet their needs, were regularly dedicated to Giles. This links with St Hugh of Lincoln who was greatly revered for his holiness and devotion, particularly for his Christian love towards lepers.

The lot of a pilgrim was hard and dangerous. What then was the inspiration? What was it that made people from all classes of society leave their homes and their homeland to undertake an arduous journey and even risk their lives? Mediaeval Christians (and most people in the western world were Christian) had a highly developed, often gruesome and technicolour doctrine of heaven and hell. Their desire was to ensure a place in heaven. As they gazed up at the intricately carved tympani above the great west doors of the churches and abbeys which so often portrayed Christ in majesty separating the sheep from the goats, their eyes would have fallen on depictions of the devil etched in stone, savage and scary. The prospect of eternal hell fire (and I am told you cannot get near the fire for clergy) was incentive enough for them to press on with their journeys. Their pilgrimage was only complete when they had touched the place where the treasured relic of the saint was kept. They believed that this close proximity to relics would aid their salvation and the particular saint would intercede on their behalf.

What then of the modern pilgrim? In our own country pilgrims have to be content with visiting the places where the relics used to be housed. In Lincoln, St Hugh's tomb was destroyed by Henry VIII and Hugh's relics have long since gone. However, a tour company recently commenting on the Cistercian way wrote "pilgrimage is a long-held tradition that remains a vibrant part of the life of many faith communities. The continued interest is a celebration of faith and gives time for reflection while creating the setting for an exciting journey of exploration. Building upon the tradition of many of Europe's best known pilgrimage routes with their mediaeval origins this new route in Wales takes as its inspiration the sacred landscapes of the Cistercians." In Lincoln people are attracted by the building itself. It is said by many to be the best gothic building north of the Alps. So what is the role of today's cathedral? It is an ecclesiastical supermarket where the shelves are loaded with all sorts of goodies. The gold standard is that cathedrals provide the best to enable the worship of God. Here is a house of prayer, a place where music is sung, liturgy celebrated, quietness and stillness encouraged, and here is a library, a place of scholarship, a centre of pastoral care, a natural setting for concerts and a nave which, when empty of chairs, is one of the best sacred spaces in Christendom. This place opens its doors to pilgrims, to the city and to the world at large. Here Rotary clubs, Women's Institutes, farmer's harvests and flower festivals are warmly welcomed and made to feel at home. This place which provides a roof for the Bishop's seat is an important place. As Philip Larkin said "it is a serious place on serious earth". The ministry of a cathedral community is crucial if all of this is to continue to be developed for the glory of God and the salvation of mankind.

Prayer

Lead us, Heavenly Father, in our pilgrimage through life. May we always be ready to face hardship and suffering for the sake of the gospel and seek those places where we find your presence. Fill us with your grace and help us to stand in awe of all that speaks of your glory and love, Amen.

Fact to Faith

At the beginning of August, we celebrate the Feast of the Transfiguration. The account of the transfiguration is very familiar when we read of Jesus with Peter, James and John ascending a mountain.

Essentially transfiguration is about a shift from fact to faith. It is at this precise moment of transfiguration that we add the name Christ to the name Jesus. Jesus is the man who was born as a baby in a stable in Bethlehem, Christ is the anointed one of God—the Son of God. The two names "Jesus Christ" bring together divinity and humanity. From the moment of our own baptism, all of us are part of and engage with this journey from humanity to divinity. This is why we follow in the steps of Jesus, the Saviour. He showed us manifestly and without doubt how the divine and the human come together in one unified and cohesive whole.

This move from fact to faith is heralded by the voice speaking from the cloud. This has a long and honorable tradition which we first come across in the account of the creation when the voice of God speaks out the words of creation. We find it again in the Abrahamic saga at the point where Abraham is about to sacrifice his son Isaac. Moses is introduced to the voice of God as he approaches the burning bush on Mt. Sinai. The theme runs through all the prophets up to the point where Jesus himself is baptised. Once again as humanity and divinity are brought together it is the voice of God which speaks at Jesus' baptism, affirming him as his beloved son.

I can never be sure whether someone who has not seen you for twenty years and tells you that you have not changed a bit, is paying you a compliment. I say this because the journey from fact to faith involves change—our prayer being that it is change for the better. So, if someone says that you look the same twenty years later, it implies that there has been no change. This is misleading because change there most certainly has been. We only need to look in the mirror to witness the change in our hair colour or, for some of us, its increasing scarcity. The journey from fact to faith, human to divine is central to the writings and thinking of the second century Irenaeus….. *'By conforming ourselves to the ordo God creates, we come to share his glory. So our "deification" is our transformation into the image of the obedient Son, the primary image of God the Father; the pledge of it is that, in spirit, we may cry "Abba Father" to God.'*

'There is "nuptial" union between God's spirit and fleshly human existence, such that the whole person is infused with the glory of God's love.' Glorification of the flesh, in other words, cannot be interpreted in a naively materialistic way—any more than it can in the case of Jesus' transfiguration (Irenaeus is the first Christian writer to use this foretype of the heavenly transformation of all believers, a theme very prominent in mediaeval Eastern writing.

This journey, then, towards God, this journey from fact to faith, from the human to the divine is also about transformation. We see this, of course in human relationships especially in marriage itself. I remember blessing a new wedding ring for a lady whose husband had died more than four years previously. She is a keen, dedicated and accomplished gardener; while gardening, she lost her ring in the soil and was unable to find it. Subsequently she then bought herself a new ring but was unhappy with it. In her words, it did not feel right. She wanted it blessed and dedicated. After the short service, she told me that she felt totally different and that the ring fitted snugly. This person is on her journey from fact to faith. It is interesting that Irenaeus should describe the union between God and humanity as "nuptial". There is nothing sadder than when the process of transformation is not mutual and you find one partner in a marriage changing more quickly than the other. Unfortunately one can be left behind and it is then that gaps begin to occur within the relationship and that sense of oneness and mutuality is under threat. Similar gaps can appear in our relationship with God as we seek to be recreated in his image and this is something that we must all guard against.

As Jesus together with Peter, James and John leaves the mountain, He orders them to tell no-one about what they have seen and experienced. Scholars have described this as the messianic secret. It seems just as soon as somebody recognises Jesus for who he is, they are ordered to keep silent. This links with the journey from fact to faith because Jesus tried his utmost not to provide proof of his identity. Proof would make faith unnecessary—tell that please to Professor Dawkin—and faith is a vital ingredient in the journey to God. It is all about believing the story and listening to the witnesses. Peter, James and John witnessed the fact of the transfiguration. When we believe their witness, then we move from fact to faith. The same occurred at Jesus' resurrection where the witness was Mary Magdalene. It is only after the experience of resurrection has been received by the twelve and it begins to filter out into the wider community that Jesus permits people to talk about his identity. The resurrection requires faith. It requires that we move from understanding things in a human way to understanding events in a divine way—we move from fact to faith. Once we have done this, then we can join in singing the words of a favourite hymn … "*Now* is eternal life if risen with Christ we stand".

The Christian faith then is about a journey; it is about being transformed and changed into the image of God; it is about moving from humanity to divinity; it is about a shift from fact to the faith. Let us pray that each of us may always continue to be transformed and transfigured into the image and glory of God.

Prayer

Lord, help us, we pray, on our journey from fact to faith. May we be ready to be transformed into your likeness so that we grow in holiness and come to share in your glory, Amen.

Mental Health and Exorcism

Before retiring as Archdeacon of Lincoln, my day usually began about six; after a cup of tea, I was ready to take the dog for a walk. Sometimes we went round the local streets and other times along by the river at Cogglesford Mill in Sleaford. What we always did was arrive at church for morning prayer at 7.30 a.m. Saffy, our golden retriever, seemed to have a sixth sense about the interior of churches and always laid down at the head of the nave, never entering the chancel. She also recognised the Lord's Prayer towards the end of the office because she stood up ready to return home. If I was not reading, I always took the opportunity to follow the Old Testament in French and the New in Greek.

In the gospels there are many occasions when we are introduced to the Pharisees testing Jesus. As so often happens, Jesus turns the tables and takes the opportunity to teach the Pharisees about what corrupts human beings. Evil, he says, comes from within. When the word evil occurred in one of the readings from the letter to the Ephesians, John Altman (Once an East Enders actor) asked me if he had heard correctly and the days really were described as evil. If so, what was my reaction? I said that I thought evil was too strong a word to use—difficult might be better. Evil is the strongest word we have in the English language for all things bad and unlawful.

Evil comes from within us, said Jesus but interestingly when he talks of evil spirits, he describes an external source for evil. In our society today we tend to internalise our demons and not rely upon the idea of some exterior force, like the devil. Naturally internalising our demons in this way makes a direct connection with mental health. Moreover, there are those who say that the list of evil intentions Jesus describes leads to the actions of a psychopath who is a person who has no insight into the difference between right and wrong.

My last attendance at the General Synod coincided with a debate on mental health which I led.

The motion before the Synod was as follows:

'That this Synod:

(a) affirm the vital necessity of improving services, in hospitals and in the community, for the care and treatment of people with mental health problems;

(b) welcome the acceptance by Her Majesty's Government during the passage of the Mental Health Act 2007 of amendments to protect the liberty and interests of those subject to compulsory detention and treatment for mental disorder, and express the hope that the operation of the Act will be carefully monitored;

(c) note with concern the rising incidence of mental distress among young people;

(d) call attention to the acute needs of people with mental disorders in the criminal justice system and request effective measures to divert them, where appropriate, from prison; and

(e) welcome the recognition within mental health services of the significance of spirituality for assessment and treatment, and encourage parishes to ensure that the support and care of people with mental health problems, their carers and NHS staff is a key priority for the Church's ministry.'

During the debate there were some excellent speeches not least from the Bishop of St Albans who asked: Why there is no heroic figure of the stature of Nightingale, Wilberforce or Fry associated with caring for the mentally ill. He said: "If I mentioned Wilberforce you would respond immediately with 'slavery' or Fry and you would talk of prisons, or Nightingale and you would respond 'hospital'. There is no such person I can think of, about whom we would then say 'mental health.'

"Why aren't there? Possibly because we have complex highly difficult relationships with mental illness. Possibly because mental illness can challenge some of our more simplistic understandings of what it is to be human and what it means to be ill and what it means to be well."

Having the opportunity to follow Old Testament readings in French, I have noticed the way in which the meaning of words can change. So, for example, the French word for a burnt offering is "holocaust". When it comes to demons and demon possession, the French word means to 'hunt'. I much prefer the idea of hunting demons rather than exorcising them. Exorcism suggests some battle between good and evil, declaring warfare on the Devil and objectifying evil as an independent force. Now this I find very difficult indeed because I cannot conceive of some objective independent demon force. At the same time my question to the exorcist is "what do you do next if the exorcism does not work?" So I much prefer the idea of hunting out and exposing demons which can then be dealt with in a therapeutic way.

There are many churches now which hold regular healing services and in most dioceses there are Healing and Deliverance teams. When a team is undertaking deliverance work almost without fail the people involved express gratitude for being taken seriously. So often they will say that family members, friends and even local doctors are neither helpful nor supportive but disbelieve them. Sometimes they are told that what they have experienced is in their imagination or that they are being foolish, dramatic or simply wanting to draw attention to themselves or worse that they are mentally ill.

Teams often include consultant psychiatrists who provide valuable insights to help make that vital distinction between the paranormal and mental illness. Diocesan teams provide a resource for parishes which are developing and expanding their own healing ministry both through healing services and pastoral care.

It is high time the church rediscovered its healing ministry. Annual conferences are now planned in most dioceses and there will be workshops on:

- Spiritual direction
- Psychotherapy
- Christian Listening
- Occupational Therapy.

I started at the beginning of the day, taking the dog for a walk. It is usually only towards the end of the day that there is time to read. Let me leave you with a verse from Act IV Scene ii of Shakespeare's Cymbeline:

"No exorciser harm thee,
Nor no witch-craft charm thee.
Ghost unlaid forbear thee.
Nothing ill come near thee.
Quiet consumption have
And renowned be thy grave."

Education Sunday 1

Today is Education Sunday more of which later. From a reading of the synoptic gospels you would be forgiven for thinking that Jesus' identity was a secret. After the Transfiguration Jesus tells Peter, James and John not to reveal who he is, which scholars have described as the 'Messianic secret'. The public religion of Jesus' time was Judaism and in today's gospel we find Jesus in the synagogue. He was familiar with the Nazareth synagogue because it was not only the place where he prayed on the Sabbath but also where, as a boy, he had learned to read. It was his school and what he did not learn here, he learnt from his Mother. There would have been men there who had been his classmates and shared his early life.

People in the congregation would have heard that Jesus had made a stir in Galilee after his baptism in the river Jordan. Now they were to hear the 'local lad' for themselves.

Any adult male could be asked to read the lesson, choosing their own passage and when Jesus began reading from Isaiah, some would have recognised that the passage included 'a day of vengeance of our God'. Jesus, however, stopped before he reached what they must have thought was the best bit!

The kingdom of God which Jesus announced was not about wreaking vengeance on the Romans. His teaching aim, which not even his chosen disciples understood (Acts 1.6), was to stretch their minds and hearts to receive what Isaiah describes as God's 'new thing' (Isaiah 43.19).

Once the young church had moved beyond the boundaries of Palestine, it was not to become the publically recognised religion of the Roman empire until the 4th. century when the Emperor Constantine decreed it. Until then, it had suffered great persecution and was often practised in the privacy of people's homes.

Christianity has remained a public religion until this day and, as you know, our own Church of England is by law established. Now, however, we are facing the serious possibility that our faith might be increasingly becoming privatised and not given the public voice and persona it has had for a very long time.

There are so many examples—viz. the diminishing of Christmas and introduction of winter festivals. Added to which, there are subtle changes to the roles people play. This Christmas outside our local Tesco store, people were collecting for a local charity. One of the collectors was dressed as Father Christmas. Now I had always thought he *gave* presents, rather than *took* your money!

On another occasion Melanie and I were in a large store where she was enjoying some retail therapy and I was looking for some Christmas cards because we had run out. I could not find a single card with pictures of the nativity. It was all snow and robins, landscapes and old masters.

Lastly (and you probably have innumerable examples of your own) Bentley cars have sacked their chaplain because it might have offended people of other faiths, though nobody from another faith had actually complained. I find this all very confusing and cannot reconcile the huge amount the church undertakes and promotes in the public arena with the creeping marginalisation and privatisation of the church.

On Education Sunday it is worth remembering that the education of Western Christendom was preserved and developed by the monasteries and that today in our country the Church of England is the largest provider of schools in the country. There are nearly 4,500 Church of England primary and middle schools and more than 190 secondary schools and now academies. Nearly one in five primary school children are educated in Church of England primary schools by 19% of all primary teachers. These schools are either voluntary controlled or voluntary aided. If the latter, then the local church is contributing financially to the schools.

This is just one example of the church's involvement in the public life of the nation. Another might be chaplaincies in the forces, prisons and hospitals. The list of examples of the church's public interaction is very long indeed.

Ours is a public faith, not a private one. The central theological truth of the Epiphany is that Jesus Christ is a universal figure. He is a person for all times, all people and all places. Our task is to ensure that the church retains its public place and public voice so that it can continue to minister to all people whoever they are and wherever they are, Amen.

Education Sunday 2

Whenever I bless children at the Communion rail, I always kneel down so that I am at the same height as they are. It is far less intimidating; and an insight I learnt from Jack Nicholls when he was Bishop of Sheffield. He was telling his wife about the time when he was visiting the reception class in a primary school and all the children were sitting on the floor. Well, she said, I hope you sat on the floor with them so that you were at their level and not 6 feet above them.

Today is Education Sunday and the gospel is from that great tract of teaching in St Matthew's gospel known as the sermon on the Mount. At the beginning we read that Jesus sat down with the people sitting on the grass around him. He did this not because he too had heard Jack Nicholls but because sitting down was how the Rabbis taught. Jesus was a Rabbi, a Jewish teacher, and identified with them in this way. Like all good teachers he was a great story teller. His stories were parables— earthly stories with a heavenly meaning; or as one child wrote 'a heavenly story with no earthly meaning'. He also used to good effect visual aids around him like the fig tree. In these and other ways Jesus kept the concentration of his listeners without relying on a microphone—lollipop or lapel.

Context is vital and we need to remind ourselves of the context for many of today's children. In the 5 to 16 age range:

- 8/10 have a TV
- 7/10 their have own computer
- 7/10 have their own internet
- 2/3 have a mobile phone

This means that they live in an electronic and virtual age. It is a very privatised way of living, a place where people increasingly live in a world of their own. Perhaps traditional ways of teaching and communicating need to be rethought and this may even include the weekly sermon.

Add to this recent research by Richard Watson who is an English research fellow working in Australia. Two years ago he predicted that in 2009 there would be a huge banking crisis which would be felt across the world. He has since suggested 10 things that, in his view, are on the way out:

- dining rooms
- letter writing on paper
- paper statements and bills
- optimism about the future
- individual responsibility
- intimacy
- humility
- concentration
- retirement
- privacy

The challenge is enormous, even more so when the latest research indicates that children have a concentration span of just 7 minutes and then boredom sets in.

Another aspect of the context is that today's children live in a multi cultural and multi faith society. In the mix are church schools which on any reckoning are the most popular, a theme the sit.com. 'Rev' humorously depicted. Paradoxically there is at least one C of E school where the children are 100% Moslem. The head teacher has to be inventive when, according to the law of the land, there has to be an act of christian worship each day. A recent Ofsted report said 'Secondary schools with a religious foundation contribute significantly and substantially more to the promotion of community cohesion and the provision of the equality of opportunity for students than other schools.'

Surprisingly even now Religious Education is the only subject that *has* to be taught in schools.

The challenge then is enormous and it is likely that there will be a shift away from specific faiths to the wider context of *spirituality*. There are officially 9 main faith communities in the U.K. viz.

- Bahai
- Buddhism
- Christianity
- Hindu
- Jain
- Judaism
- Islam
- Sikhism
- Zoroastrianism

It is said that spirituality is a bridge between faith communities and post-modern people. Gary Hartz the American commentator has written 'in the midst of disillusionment and alienation, many find themselves thirsting for spiritual experiences and religious community.'

Spirituality can encompass a vast spread of phenomena viz: Values, Meaning, Trust, Compassion, Vision, Hope, Transcendence, Love, Forgiveness, Origins, Purpose, Being human, Mystery, Holiness, Glory.

That said, world religions and faith communities which are incorporated within spirituality still provide:
- The sacred
- Moral codes
- Institutions
- Communities

The task for the christian church is to discover/rediscover its spirituality which surely must centre on the person of Jesus. At the same time the churches need to ensure that they offer the world:

A welcome and acceptance

- Social networks
- Supportive Communities
- Reconciliation and Healing
- Worship and Prayer

The challenge is great both for the churches and for those who have dedicated their lives to education but, at the same time, it is the mission of the church in the world. Remember Jesus died not to save the church but the world.

Battle of Britain

Like most people I do not particularly like being in a confined space. My most memorable experience of such a space was when Melanie and I visited the Battle of Britain Memorial Flight at RAF Coningsby. Today the flight usually consists of a Hawker Hurrican, an Avro Lancaster and a Supermarine Spitfire. The Lancaster bomber did not come into service until 1945; the bomber most used in the Battle of Britain was the Blenheim.

I was invited to crawl through the fuselage of the Lancaster to the place occupied by the forward gunner. It was so small that it was not even possible to turn round but simply to lie stretched out. Little wonder that both forward and rear gunners were so vulnerable to enemy fire. Today the Memorial Flight of a bomber and two fighters which are nearly 75 years old, are in continual demand to fly at a variety of events throughout the U.K.

Today is Battle of Britain Sunday and the name derives from a famous speech delivered by Prime Minister Winston Churchill in the House of Commons: "...the Battle of France is over. I expect that the Battle of Britain is about to begin."

The Battle of Britain was the first major campaign to be fought entirely by air forces, and was also the largest and most sustained aerial bombing campaign to that date. From July 1940 coastal shipping convoys and shipping centres, such as Portsmouth, were the main targets of the German Air Force; one month later the *Luftwaffe* shifted its attacks to RAF airfields and their infrastructure. As the battle progressed the *Luftwaffe* also targeted aircraft factories and the infrastructure of cities and towns in the South of England. Eventually the *Luftwaffe* resorted to attacking areas of political significance concentrating particularly on London.

The failure of Germany to achieve its objectives of destroying Britain's air defences, or forcing Britain to negotiate an armistice or an outright surrender, is considered its first major defeat and one of the crucial turning points in the war. If Germany had gained air superiority over England, Hitler might have launched Operation Sea Lion, an amphibious and airborne invasion of Britain.

Air superiority was essential for the Germans because the Royal Navy still had 50 destroyers, 21 cruisers and eight battle ships in the British Home Fleet. There was little the weakened German navy could do to prevent the Royal Navy intervening in a proposed German invasion.

Air Chief Marshall Sir H.C.T. "Stuffy" Dowding not only had his own strategy for RAF Fighter Command which he commanded but also the use of Radio Direction Finding—later known as radar.

As an invasion became more likely, Coastal Command participated in the strikes on French harbours and airfields, laying mines, and mounting numerous reconnaissance missions over the enemy-held coast. In all, some 9180 sorties were flown by bombers from July to October 1940. Although this was much less than the 80,000 sorties flown by fighters, bomber crews suffered about half the total number of casualties borne by their fighter colleagues. The Battle of Britain was the more amazing because the RAF was outnumbered 5 to 1 by the Luftwaffe. During the battle and for the rest of the war public morale was sustained because the King and Queen determined to stay in London. On the 10 and 13 September, Buckingham Palace was bombed and the Royal Chapel was destroyed. The Queen was later to say that she could now look the East End in the face.

It was Churchill who summed up the effect of the battle and the part played by Fighter Command in the immortal words "Never in the field of human conflict was so much owed by so many to so few". The name *The Few* was later given to the pilots who fought in the Battle of Britain.

The idea of the few as a remnant has always had a very respectable place in biblical theology. It began with Noah who was charged with preserving life with the few gathered in the ark. It reached its zenith with the exile to Babylon and in the person of Jesus was given a new meaning in New Testament theology. The notion is that God will always provide a remnant— the few—to continue the story of salvation and how He engages with humanity.

The story of Noah and the ark is a symbolic picture of the inevitable consequences of the rejection of the rule of God. Man is overwhelmed by the disorder which he himself has created; but God's purpose for blessing is undefeated, and the principle of the remnant, which was to play so important a part in the development of that purpose, emerges from the wreck, and the way is prepared for a new beginning. Amos adds to the hope in Chapter 9..."I will destroy this sinful kingdom from off the face of the earth; saving that I will not *utterly* destroy the house of Jacob".

Turn to Isaiah and the threat is not external like floods or German aircraft but the destruction of holiness. The disciplining of the nation would not wholly consume it, but would leave a remnant to carry on its life and to inherit its promises.

In Micah, the remnant is seen as totally victorious over the nations of the world throughout which Israel has been dispersed. This dispersion of the Jewish people continues to this day. It was the group known as the Hasidaeans who represented, in an almost literal sense, the remnant of the nation which was to carry forward the great religious tradition of Israel's past.

When we come to the New Testament, the prophetic doctrine of the remnant called for a leader qualified morally and spiritually to lead such a redemptive community and that person is Jesus. There can be no doubt that Jesus also had in mind his small band of disciples as a remnant whose corporate experience of fellowship with one another and with Jesus as their Lord and Master was to be instrumental in ushering in the kingdom of God. The 12 were forerunners of the church and consequently a feature of the church is that it too is called upon to be a remnant actively at work in the world.

Whatever the vicissitudes are that prevail against the Church, the doctrine of the remnant asserts that there will always be enough committed Christians to continue its life and future.

Some commentators speak the language of the 'remnant' today citing the attacks on the established church and the 'dumbing down' of the Christian faith from daily worship in schools to wearing Christian symbols and to no religious services being broadcast on television on Christmas one year. If a remnant is needed again, then rest assured that God will provide the resources for the church to continue its mission and ministry through the few.

Prayer

We are ever mindful of the sacrifices made by those who were involved in the last World War to secure freedom and democracy so that we might live in peace today. We thank you, good Lord, for your promise always to provide a remnant to carry forward the truths and traditions of the past and so enable the rumour of God to be kept alive, Amen.

Angels and Archangels

Imagine for a moment you are Medieval pilgrim. It is the 12th Century and you have decided along with one or two others from your village that you are going to make a pilgrimage to Santiago de Compostella in North Western Spain. If you manage to complete this dangerous and arduous journey, you will be ensured of a more favourable judgement when your time comes. As importantly, because you have gazed upon the relics of St James and perhaps even touched the golden box that contains them, you have it on the word of Holy Mother Church that St James will ever intercede on your behalf. The first choice of you and your fellow pilgrims was not Santiago but Jerusalem— the birthplace of Christianity. Unfortunately the Wars of the Crusades are being fought there and a pilgrimage is out of the question. It was then that you all discussed whether you should go to St Peter's tomb in Rome or to Santiago. You all eventually decided on Compostella and are now ready to leave and travel by foot and by boat to this far away place. It could take a year or even two. Just getting out of England will be bad enough without the crossing of the channel in some leaky wooden boat and then all the way through France, over the Pyrennees and along the North Coast of Spain—the first route the pilgrims took because of the Muslim threat from the South.

You have all heard from others who have made the journey before you of the wonderful abbeys and cathedrals you will visit on the way. Here the monks and nuns will provide food and shelter and somewhere to rest. You may well look up at some of the tympani above the great west doors of the stunning Romanesque buildings. Delicately carved in stone you will see depictions of the Last Judgement. Here the sheep are divided from the goats. The jaws of Hell remain open to receive the damned and the angels around the throne of Heaven hold out welcoming hands to the blessed. It's all very dramatic and not a little spooky.

Chief among the angels is Michael, an archangel. Michael, Gabriel and Raphael are the three named biblical angels depicted as the beloved messengers of God. Michael, which means 'who is like God', is described as protector of Israel and leader of the armies of God and is perhaps best known as the slayer of the dragon in the Revelation of St John. He is thus regarded as the protector of Christians from the devil, particularly those at the hour of death. A basilica near Rome was dedicated in the 5th century in honour of Michael on 30 September, beginning with celebrations on the eve of that day, and 29 September is now kept in honour of Michael and all Angels throughout the Western Church.

So there are angels in the Bible; people have experienced the presemce of angels and what angels do is to attend to our inner lives. Each of us has an inner and outer life. In the 14th Century there was a woman called Julian, though this is not her real name but one taken from the dedication of the church. Living in a cell attached to the Church of St Julian in Norwich. This place was at the centre of her spiritual life, her inner life, her life with God—it was here that she listened to the voice of God and it was here that she spoke to God. It was in this place that she experienced the divine presence and the touch of God upon her life. In her cell she was free to dream, to imagine, to have visions, to let her mind drift beyond the immediate and visible to the eternal and the hidden. These devout practices nourished and kept alive within her the Christian faith and the divine spark which was her gift from God. It is this vision of God, this experience of the Divine, the mystery, otherness and holiness that we seek to offer to the world. Our task is to share with people that great truth that Jesus died for the world. This was all part of the inner life of Julian of Norwich which she lived out her life within the confines of the four walls of her cell. Some might have called her an angel and it is certainly true that there are people whom others call angels. It is a term, commonly associated with nurses and I am sure that there are people whom you have known whom you would describe as angels.

Angels have three roles. They are guardians, messengers and worshipers. It is said that each of us has a guardian angel who cares for us, particularly spiritually, who values us and who is concerned for us as individual people.

The main function of angels in the Bible was to be messengers and this is exemplified by Gabriel who gives the news to Mary that she is to be the mother of Jesus. Lastly it is angels who surround the heavenly throne worshiping God. We are reminded of this at every service of Holy Communion when we hear the words 'Therefore with angels and archangels and with the whole company of Heaven we laud and magnify thy name ever praising thee and saying …..' We then say or sing the words the angels sing in Heaven—Holy, Holy, Holy Lord God of Hosts.

The threefold function of angels is surely what each and every one of us should attain to. We too are to be guardians, messengers and worshipers. We too are to have a care for other people, relay the message of the Gospel and be faithful in worship. Be thankful for the angels and be ready to be an angel and always a part of the worship of the Almighty God.

Prayer

Be with us, we pray, on our pilgrimage through this life and may we always be protected by your heavenly angels. May we, like them, have a care for other people, relay the message of the Gospel and be faithful in worship, ever praising your Holy Name, Amen.

Harvest

(Leviticus 19 vs 9)
'When you reap the harvest of your land, do not reap to the
very edges of your field or gather the gleanings of your harvest.'

The last funeral I conducted was for a man of 93. Born at the turn
of the last century this person had probably seen more changes
in his lifetime than at any other time in human history. He had
seen, for example, reliance on the horse change to reliance on
the motor car. He had seen vast developments in communication
systems from the telephone to the Internet. As a Norfolk farmer,
he had seen nothing less than a phenomenal change in farming,
agricultural machinery and the agro-chemical industry. Those
changes continue today and, like the 93 year old farmer, not
only do we experience them but we also have to accommodate
them. For example, food mountains have given way to set aside.
Set aside, as it is practised today, is designed to take land out
of production. At first, this may appear to be a rather negative
response to over-production, simply leaving to one side land to
become fallow. However, there is a positive side as well because
often set aside land has new trees planted on it or it is allowed
to develop naturally which provides new habitats for wild life
and flora. The passage which I have just quoted from the book of
Leviticus suggests that a form of set aside was being practised by
the ancient Jews, so much so that it became built into their legal
system. It was established in law that farmers should not harvest
to the very edges of the field but set this land aside. Again, you
could say that this was a negative thing to do and a waste of a
good crop. On the other hand, it is very clear that not only was
it positive but also contributed to social welfare and the care of
others in the community. Corn and grapes which were left at the
edges of the fields were set aside for those who in ancient Israel

were identified as the poor and needy. They were the widows and orphans and aliens, foreigners from other countries. As we learned in the first lesson, not only were the poor of those times invited to take the crops from the edges of the fields but also to go gleaning after the harvest had been gathered in.

The practice of not harvesting the edges of the field has been discontinued today but we certainly need to find a twentieth century equivalent. However, there are many farmers who still encourage people to glean. Once the potato harvester or bean harvester has finished its work in the fields, local people are invited to pick up any of the crops that have been left behind by the harvesters. I well remember a person in the village where I used to live gathering three whole sacks of potatoes long after the potato harvester had left. It was enough to keep the family in potatoes, he told me, until Christmas.

Land that is set aside and crops that are set aside can both make a valuable and positive contribution to the world in which we live and to the people who inhabit it. Even with set aside, there is still more than enough food in this country for all of us to be adequately supplied. Year by year we meet to thank the creator, God, for the fruits of the earth. We sing 'All good gifts around us are sent from heaven above, then praise the Lord, O praise the Lord, for all his love.' Similarly, year by year, we can say this with conviction for we are blessed by God who does supply our wants and needs. In Lincolnshire, people are conscious of not just the fruits of the fields but also the wide variety of vegetables which are grown on the very rich reclaimed land in the east of the county. Fruit, vegetables and corn are in abundance and it is both right and proper that we see the hand of God in all this.

As well as not harvesting right to the edges of the field and as well as set aside, at harvest time we also need to be aware of people who are set aside. There are many reasons why in modern society people are pushed to the edges and become, what is called, marginalised. People, for example, with disabilities who may be confined to a wheelchair are marginalised often because they cannot gain access to buildings and this includes churches. There are people who are unemployed and have been for many years with no hope or prospect of further work. Not only does this have a devastating effect upon many of them but somehow they are thought to be blameworthy for the situation in which they find themselves and, because they are restricted to state benefits, are moving imperceptibly towards the edges of society. There are many groups of people, some of them well known, some of them less well known. Let me just identify two groups—those with mental health problems and learning disabilities. Again, they are set aside and find themselves living within the shadows of society. It is a twilight existence, full of uncertainty, risk and, so very often, painful loneliness. Set aside people are the poor, the needy and vulnerable who live near the margins and occupy those places which are at the edges of the community. There are, however, other groups of people who are set aside in a much more positive way. It is said that priests are called to be set aside from society in order better to pray for it and serve it. Priests are to be people who are in the world, but not of the world. If, like me, you believe in the priesthood of all believers, it is but a short step to say that this idea of positive set aside applies not just to priests but to all christian people, old and young alike. So we could say that the Church itself is an organisation set aside to be in the world but not of the world and this is because it sets its sights on something that is higher and beyond mere human experience and existence. The Church is called to be a vehicle of the eternal, to be a means of expressing the presence of God in the world and a way of understanding the deep mysteries of God and his love for people. This will involve the Church in building up community life, strengthening family ties, pursuing goodness, demanding justice, and holding up the needs of the world in a continual prayer to God. It is only by being set aside that the Church is freed to serve the world and offer to it a vision of the eternal. All of this means that the Church is set aside to minister to those whom society at large has set aside and to do this it needs to learn again the lesson from the rule in Leviticus not to harvest right up to the edges of the field and to make sure that those in need have an opportunity to do some gleaning. In other words, the Church must encourage the world to find ways of being generous so that we begin to reflect the generosity of God himself. One of the marks of a civilised society is that it looks after its weaker members and, if we fail to do this, then what will happen is that the poor will become poorer and the vulnerable more vulnerable. It is then, though if we have already arrived at that point, it is now that we need to remind ourselves of a question which David Jenkins asked. David Jenkins was the previous Bishop of Durham and his question was 'What are we in the process of becoming?' The answer to that question should be that we are in the process of becoming reflections of the love of God, living up to the image in which he created us and seeking to become more divine moment by moment. I fear that, unless we learn the message of the generosity of the harvest, we shall become a poorer and a sadder place. Let us then ensure that at least we, when we reap the harvest of our land, do not reap to the very edges of our fields or gather the gleanings of our harvest. We are not to go over our vineyards a second time or pick up the grapes that have fallen. Leave them for the poor and the alien and the needy. This is the word of the Lord, your God, Amen.

Prayer

Lord God of the harvest, may we ever be thankful for the food we enjoy day by day and month by month. Help us to take every opportunity to support those whose harvests have failed and who will not have enough to sustain them, Amen.

St Faith

When Melanie and I visited St Faith's former abbey church at Conques in the Aveyron we were surprised to discover that it was smaller than we had anticipated. It is in a very remote part of the countryside on the way to Southern France but the setting is idyllic. As we entered through the south door, we were greeted by the sound of a piano being played beautifully and the music emanated from the dark shadows of the crossing at the head of the nave. It was lovely to take a day out of our holiday and spend it in this wonderful building which gives its name to your Patron Saint.

Faith was a virgin and martyr. 'The martyrology of Jerome records her death at Agen in Gaul, so it is good to know that it is likely that she really existed. However, her legend is quite unhistorical; she was further confused with the mythical sisters Faith, Hope and Charity and their mother Sophia. The diffusion of her cult in the Middle Ages was remarkable. Her body was translated to Conques, where the justly famous reliquary in the 10th Century survives, a masterpiece of barbaric Dark Ages art. Here both Crusaders and pilgrims to the shrine of St James at Compostella invoked her intercession and took back the memory of her to their own countries. In many districts of France are found place names and church dedications to Sainte Foy. In England a shrine of the saint was set up at Horsham St Faith, near Norwich. Her fame past not only to Italy and Spain but also eventually to South America especially Bogota. In England, chapels were dedicated to her in Westminster Abbey and St Paul's Cathedral and no fewer than 23 ancient English churches also were consecrated in her name. The historical records indicate that she was a young girl who was put to death by being roasted on a brazen bed and then beheaded. This inspired numerous artistic representations of her, in which a sword or a bundle of rods is her emblem. She soon became the Patron of soldiers, prisoners and pilgrims who invoked her patronage and asked for her prayers.' (The Oxford Dictionary of Saints)

When there were monks living here in the Middle Ages, Conques was a centre of pilgrimage. Imagine, for a moment, that you are a Medieval pilgrim and transport yourself a thousand years back to the days when this abbey church was bustling with monks going about their business of worship, study, prayer, and the daily life of the monastery.

It is the 12th Century and you have decided along with one or two others from Gaywood that you are going to make a pilgrimage to Santiago de Compostella in North Western Spain. If you manage to complete this dangerous and arduous journey, you will be ensured of a more favourable last judgement when your time comes. As importantly, because you have gazed upon the relics of St James (Sant-Iago) and perhaps even touched the golden box that contains them, you have it on the word of Holy Mother Church that St James will ever intercede on your behalf. The first choice for you and your fellow pilgrims was not Santiago but Jerusalem—the birthplace of Christianity. Unfortunately the Wars of the Crusades are being fought there and a pilgrimage is out of the question. It was then that you all discussed whether you should go to St Peter's tomb in Rome or to Santiago. You all eventually decided on Compostella and are now ready to leave Gaywood and travel by foot and by boat to this far away place. It could take a year or even two. Just getting out of Norfolk will be bad enough without the crossing of the Channel in some leaky wooden boat and then all the way through France, over the Pyrenees and along the North Coast of Spain—the first route the pilgrims took because of the Muslim threat from the South.

When you reach Roncesvalles, you will be joined by other

pilgrims who followed the route from Vezelay and those who came from Le Puy. It is this route the third of four which passes through Conques.

You have all heard from others who have made the journey before you about the wonderful abbeys and cathedrals you will visit on the way. Here the monks and nuns will provide food and shelter and somewhere to rest. You may well look up at some of the tympani above the great west doors of the stunning Romanesque buildings. Delicately carved in stone you will see depictions of the Last Judgement. Here the sheep are divided from the goats. The jaws of Hell remain open to receive the damned and the angels around the throne of Heaven hold out welcoming hands to the blessed. It's all very dramatic and not a little spooky.

You may well get into conversation with some of the pilgrims who have come from the Massif Centrale through Conques who will describe to you the wonderful sculpture on the tympanum which was carved in the 1140s.

In contrast to Beaulieu, Christ in Conques is a strict judge who divides the world beyond into Heaven and Hell.

Along with pilgrims who have come across France from neighbouring countries including places as far away as Scandinavia, as you approach the Spanish Border, the conversation turns to Compostella.

The name Compostella is often said to be a corruption of Campus Stellae or 'field of the star' and so refers to the way in which the tomb had been found. An alternative explanation is that it derived from the Latin word for a cemetery. However, all of this is part of the legend and the belief that St James was buried at Compostella. This is important because it would mean he was the only apostle to be buried in western Europe outside Rome.

The four pilgrimage routes were described in a remarkable

document compiled in the 1130s. It was really an early guidebook and gave practical information on some of the hazards pilgrims would meet, the nature of the regions through which they would travel, the people who inhabited them, and the important shrines en route, including a detailed description of the cathedral in Santiago as it was at that time. The traditional pilgrim's equipment consisted of a broad-brimmed hat, a long cloak, a small pouch or scrip for some food and personal belongings, a gourd or something similar to carry water, sandals and a long staff tipped by an iron ferrule to serve both as a walking stick and as a weapon in case of attack. It was only after they reached Santiago that pilgrims were entitled to wear the cockleshell which was the symbol of the pilgrim.

Here is a wealth of history and today we stand in this amazing tradition of these devout people who undertook pilgrimages to far away parts of the world. The practice continues today so what then of the modern pilgrim?

In our own country pilgrims have to be content with visiting the places where the relics used to be housed. For example, in Lincoln, St Hugh's tomb was destroyed by Henry VIII and his relics have long since gone. However, a tour company recently commenting on the Cistercian way wrote "pilgrimage is a long-held tradition that remains a vibrant part of the life of many faith communities. The continued interest is a celebration of faith and gives time for reflection while creating the setting for an exciting journey of exploration. Building upon the tradition of many of Europe's best known pilgrimage routes with their mediaeval origins this new route in Wales takes as its inspiration the sacred landscapes of the Cistercians."

I remember pilgrims coming through Gaywood on their way to the catholic shrine at Walsingham on the Wednesday of Holy Week. They slept the night in the church hall and always came to Holy Communion the following morning.

I hope that each and every one of you will continue to embrace the concept of pilgrimage and I know that some of you have been Conques, to other pilgrimage centres abroad and to places of holiness and mystery like Lindisfarne and Walsingham in the UK. These places are in Philip Larkin's words 'serious places on serious earth'. They are important because they speak of the mystery, the glory and the presence of God. It is here that we are touched by the hand of God, enthused with divine grace and invited to kneel in the presence of God and commit ourselves through Jesus to him.

Prayer

Dear Lord, be with us on our pilgrimage through life. We pray that you will be behind us to support us, alongside us to accompany us, ahead of us to guide us, and above us to bless us, Amen.

World Mental Health Day

Across the world in thousands of different churches, communities and sacred places, people have come together to talk about and reflect upon mental health. Every year the 10th October is designated as World Mental Health day. This year the day happens to fall on a Sunday.

Let me then begin by congratulating all of you here in Salisbury Cathedral who have planned this service for ensuring that mental health and the many issues associated with it are brought to people's attention and to thank the Dean and Chapter for incorporating World Mental Health day into the Cathedral's Sunday morning Eucharist. I am grateful for the invitation to preach this morning and for the opportunity to continue our conversation after the service over coffee.

For centuries mental health has been a Cinderella service both under-funded and at the bottom on any priority list. The only exception to this was in Victorian times when a huge building programme was completed so that every city and every county had its own asylum. In the last 25 years these large hospitals have almost all been closed because so many people are now being supported in the community.

Yet the figures are startling and there are a host of statistics. Let me give you just a few:

- It was predicted that by 2020 depression would be the most prevalent illness after coronary heart disease. This year it has already happened.
- 1:4 people will suffer from a mental illness at sometime in their lifetime.
- 1:100 people suffer from schizophrenia.
- Suicide is the second most common cause of death in men under 35.

- 3/4 million people in the U.K. suffer from dementia.
- In 1985, 2/3 of all hospital beds were in psychiatric hospitals. Today less than a 1/4 are in psychiatric units. The *2/3 figure* has simply moved from the hospital to the community.
- Equally daunting are the prison figures—In 1985 the prison population was 40,000. It is now more than 90,000 and 70% of the prison population has a mental illness –among whom there are 5000 people with a severe and enduring mental illness which is a terrible scandal. Unsurprisingly then there are many who say that the prisons have become the new asylums.
- Finally there is growing concern about the number of young people and children who have mental health problems. The figure is 1:10 .

There are only 3 ways in which your liberty can be removed. The first is illegal immigration, the second offences against the law which lead to arrest and the third a mental illness which renders a person a danger to themselves or other people, or if treatment is required. To deprive a person of their liberty by detaining them under the mental health act is a huge step to take and must only be a last resort. The legislation excludes drugs, alcohol and sexual deviancy. This means, for example, that paedophilia is not a mental illness. Not to have these exclusions could mean that psychiatrists become agents of social control, as has happened in other countries. You will appreciate that there are some crucial ethical issues involved in detention under the mental health act. For example, there is the balance to be struck between individual liberty and public safety.

As well as all the statistics which record the vast numbers of people who suffer with mental health problems, there is the plight of the sufferer who is often stigmatized and socially excluded. In fact there are 4 groups who suffer particularly and who are over represented in mental health statistics:

- People from black and ethnic minority groups,
- Offenders,
- Women,
- Homeless people.

Today's Gospel read by the Canon Treasurer and last night's second lesson at Evensong introduced us to the Gedarene who had been excluded from his local community because he was too difficult to manage. He had broken loose from the chains which were used to restrict him and he lived among the tombs in the churchyard. He also self- abused using sharp stones to cut himself and shouted out to his minders and anyone who came near. His name was Legion because 'there are so many of us'. This might refer to a multiple personality or to voices he heard. Today he would be classified as suffering from a psychotic illness or a personality disorder. His own inner life was in turmoil and he was constantly confronting his demons which plagued him night and day. Into this scene steps Jesus who earlier had himself been accused by the doctors of the law of being possessed. Jesus arrived with his apostles by boat from the other side of Lake Galilee. As Jesus came close to Legion, he showed no fear. Fear is a common reaction when people meet mental illness for the first time. Rather Jesus engaged Legion in conversation, asking him his name. He then heals him and Legion's inner chaos is transferred to a herd of pigs which career down the hillside into the sea. What followed is one of the most beautiful descriptions in the whole of the Bible. There was Jesus with Legion who was 'sitting clothed and in his right mind'. Understandably, Legion asks Jesus if he can join him. Jesus tells him to return to his own people—the very ones who had excluded him!

There are three lessons to be learnt from this miracle. The first is Jesus' own teaching when dealing with mental illness.

Do not be afraid; and treat the person with dignity and respect by relating to them, using their name and engaging them in a conversation. The second is the healing Jesus offered Legion for his broken spirit and troubled mind. As well as care and support, there is often healing and certainly enough help to enable a person with a mental health problem to participate fully in day to day living.

Lastly, Jesus returned Legion to his own community. This is perhaps the first recorded example of community care.

The three lessons are just as relevant today. Education, healing and community care are all part of an integrated whole. Though often referred to as spirituality rather than religion, there is an increasing interest in the relationship between mental health and spirituality. Many psychiatrists include spirituality in the diagnostic process because it enables them to understand better the whole person. A holistic approach takes account of every aspect of a person' life—their cultural background, spirituality, family constellation, personality, in fact everything that impinges on a person's health.

The impact of treating the whole person is that with care, support and listening, a person is enabled to come to terms with themselves, their condition and the reality of their particular situation, all of which is crucial for a successful recovery.

In modern mental health services there is a developing role for the chaplain who, like other health professionals, often works with a team of colleagues. The chaplain is there to offer pastoral care to both patients and staff and to provide a ministry to the whole organization. It is the chaplain who builds links with the community, especially with local churches, mosques and temples. Essential to the recovery process in psychiatry is the provision of time and space and this is another aspect of the chaplain's work. Do please pray for and support your own chaplains who, like many other clergy, work in a world where Christianity and religious faith struggle against unbearably relentless secularism and atheism.

The latest government initiative in mental health is called 'New Horizons' which stresses the importance of housing and education among the resources which are necessary for recovery from mental illness. Someone with mental health problems does not usually ask for much. It has been said that the basic requirements are:

- A roof over your head,
- A job,
- A date at the weekend.

Here the local church has an important and critical role to play. Not only can it make its buildings available where people with mental health problems can meet and become more integrated and where they can find asylum, but it can also provide:

- A welcome to people who often experience loneliness and isolation.
- Social networks as part of an educative process.
- A supportive community where pastoral care and friendship can be offered. For people moving in and out of reality and experiencing isolation and sometimes desperation, this type of support is vital.
- A ministry of healing which includes regular healing services, the sacraments and intercessory prayer.

More and more research is being undertaken and to date this shows, not surprisingly, that people supported by their local church community make a more rapid and successful recovery.

After a debate I led on mental health in the General Synod, a parish pack was launched for the dioceses and many churches have made use of it. It is called 'Promoting mental health: A resource for spiritual and pastoral care' and is still available today. I still have a few and will leave one here in the Cathedral.

Finally, cathedrals have a unique part to play in the support of people with mental health problems. They are accessible because they are open everyday and they offer a place of quietness and anonymity which can be a prerequisite for someone who is fearful of how they will be received. It is the Psalmist who writes:

> *I am forgotten like one that is dead, out of mind;*
> *I have become like a broken vessel.*
> (Psalm 31 vs.12)

Sufferers are only too well aware of the stigma associated with mental illness and the strange ideas some people have about it. They are afraid and uncertain and often looking for a listening ear and a place where they feel accepted.

We ought never to forget that healing is a two way process. As the healer gives of their time and skills to the sufferer, so the sufferer ministers to the healer. Roger Grainger who was a chaplain for mental health services in Wakefield wrote this:-

"We not only do people with mental health problems an injustice, when we treat them as though their interest lies in their difference from ourselves, we deprive ourselves of the life of mutuality which could exist between us if we would allow it to do so."

We all have an important part to play in the care and support of people who constitute a significant percentage of the population in this country. My prayer is that God will bless all your work and endeavours in this very important ministry, Amen.

Prayer

Be present, we pray, O lord with those who grapple with mental health problems. May the churches and society always be ready to provide healing, education and community care so that those who suffer may be able to have rich and fulfilling lives, Amen.

All Saints

The beginning of November provides an opportunity to celebrate *all* the saints. It is a lovely Festival and one of the best in the Church's calendar. This is because it provides us with a chance to think about and value all the holy people of God. There are some who are very well known like Jesus' apostles and there are others whose lives have been hidden from public view; yet they have been dedicated, holy and saintly but often known only to God. Saints are important because they are lights in their own generations, beacons of faith, examples to all of us of the holy life, and counted among those who sustain a continuous prayer for the world before God. Moreover what they do for us is threefold:-

- Their stories blend with the divine story and so keep alive for successive generations the rumour of God.
- Saints are people who have had the courage to stand firm for the truth of the gospel in adversity—so we need them today more than ever.
- Saintly lives help us to know more about holiness and more about God.

I would like to introduce two people one of whom is a saint from history who died in the year 285 AD and who is the patron saint of many churches. You may recognise him.

The other is a man who lived and died at the end of the 20th Century. He was known to only a very few people. There are no churches dedicated to him nor is he to be found in any books on the lives of contemporary saints.

The first saint is Laurence who was a deacon in the city of Rome and was martyred as a result of the persecutions by being roasted on a gridiron. His captors demanded that he brought all the treasures from the church. Laurence went inside the church where he worked and came out, to the disgust and consternation of his tormentors, with the church's treasures—a group of the poorest people from the town. This, as you may imagine, made his captors even more angry.

Laurence's story is part of the divine story because he stands courageously over against the corrupt powers of the day and, without saying a word, teaches them a gospel truth which is that real treasure is to be found in people rather than precious jewels.

The second person I came to know well when Melanie and I were living and working in the Diocese of Norwich. From 1976 onwards for the next 16 years my brief was to be the parish priest of three small villages and also the chaplain for the acute psychiatric hospitals in Norwich. As so often happens when you spend a long time in a place, you acquire other responsibilities and one of these was to be a Mental Health Act Commissioner visiting people detained in psychiatric units. This I did from 1986 to 1995 and as well as getting to know East Anglia and north east Thames very well I also visited the special hospitals—Broadmoor, Ashworth and Rampton. The work in the psychiatric units where I led an ecumenical chaplaincy team developed during this time and I had the opportunity to undertake psychotherapy. This meant receiving referrals from the doctors, the wards and other colleagues. One of the consultant psychiatrists asked if I could help with a particular patient of his who had been in the hospital for many years and whom he had discovered was a very able musician. His name was Geoffrey and I soon discovered that he played the piano, the organ (but without the pedals), the piano accordion and the mouth organ. Geoff had suffered from a mental illness for many years but, most of the time, it only affected him very mildly. There were occasions when he became quite low and preoccupied but they did not last for very long. The reason that he had become a long-term patient in the hospital was because he was also blind from birth. He really should have gone to a proper school for the blind where he could have learnt skills to enable him to live a much more independent life but, for whatever reason, this did not happen. Rather he found himself in this large hospital at a time when the policy was to move from institutional care to community care and this was the pathway that his consultant wanted to follow. I was able to help; and to cut a very long story short Geoff became the organist for one of the village churches. He had a very large repertoire of hymns, songs and pieces of music and, as long as he was given the number of verses in a hymn, the key and the first line he was more than competent in accompanying the hymn singing. There were occasions when he forgot the tune and I would have to simply stop what I was doing in the service and go and quietly sing the tune in his ear which was enough to enable him to play. Bach chorales and the like were not really his forte and so we were never quite sure what voluntary he would play at the end of a service but became used to a regular rendering of the 'Dambusters March', 'I'm Dreaming of a White Christmas' after the Christmas midnight service, the Donkey Serenade on Palm Sunday and Easter Bonnet after the Easter Day service. Geoff brought a spontaneity, a flexibility and joy to the worship and folk would be seen dancing out of church. He also had his own way of 'seeing' God and would use the keys on the piano to remind him that G stood for God and C for Christ and D for Deity and so on. He would talk quite readily about his faith and his belief in God with anyone prepared to listen and he soon became a favourite not only with the people who came to church but also the wider community.

There was one particular poignant occasion when it was time to prepare for the annual carol service. Like so many other churches we arranged for people from different groups and organisations to read the lessons and on this occasion decided to choose one of our organists. I asked Geoffrey whether he would be prepared to do this and he was delighted to be asked. I then acquired the necessary Braille which is a colossal sheet for just five verses from the bible, as you may know. I escorted him to the lectern and he placed his hands on the Braille writing and began to speak saying 'There were shepherds abiding in the fields .....'. He then very suddenly stopped speaking, apologised and said that he was sorry that he was reading so slowly but, he said, his hands were cold!

Why then do I cite Geoffrey as a saint. Was it because of the amazing way in which he overcame adversity? Was it to do with his gifts which he employed for the glory of God? Was it more about his quiet determined faithfulness? You might say it was all of these things but I would say that his saintliness resided in the fact that he was truly able to be in the world but not of the world and that perhaps, because of his mental disorder, like so many, he was able to have access to experiences denied to the rest of us. Certainly, and I think without doubt, his story is part of the divine story and there was a quality to him that was not confined to time and space but was much more to do with his own spiritual journey and ability to come close to the mystery of God.

So then, saints are important people because they teach us about holiness and prayer, about God and mystery, about the gospel and the way in which we should relate to the world around us. The saints too are to be numbered with the angels and archangels and the whole company of Heaven who eternally laud and magnify the name of God in the heavenly realms with the eternal song of praise to the one who creates, sustains, redeems, sanctifies, and glorifies each one of us.

Prayer

God, our Father, thank you for the saints and their example of holiness to us all. May we always seek to follow a life of sainthood which encourages others to see God at work in us. As we dedicate ourselves anew to a life in Christ, we pray that we may ever give thanks for the lives, examples and continued prayers of the saints for the whole world, Amen.

Bereavement

Today's service is a very special occasion. This is because it becomes part of your story. Today provides us with a moment in the story when we can pray for the person we have lost. Here is an opportunity to say thank you. This is a time to ask God to enfold the person that we grieve in his eternal embrace. Telling our story whether to God or to one another or reflectively to ourselves is central to the way in which we cope with our feelings and our grief and our sorrow.

It was the Jewish philosopher and theologian Martin Buber who was born in Vienna in 1878 and who died in Palestine in 1965, who wrote that "real meeting is in the in-between". I understand Buber to be saying that when two people meet, it is not what each individual brings to the meeting that is critical, but what ensues when the two begin to interact. Real meeting is in the in-between. Now I would like to extend Buber's perception by saying that real meeting and real healing is in the conversation. I say this because I believe that each person's story is important, valuable and vital. It is what each of us offers another person when we meet them.

Central to the Christian faith is the Bible and particularly the New Testament. In the New Testament we can read the story of Jesus and most especially his ministry as a young man. The story tellers devote a lot of their books to the last week in Jesus' life—the way he entered the city of Jerusalem in triumph but was left ignominiously to die on a cross on a green hill outside the city walls. The story does not end here nor, indeed, in a garden on Easter day morning but outside the city of Jerusalem on a hill where Jesus finally left his friends, the Apostles. Even now this is not the end of the story because the pages in the New Testament which follow tell of the emergence of the infant church as it struggles for its identity and its existence. Not only do we find stories about Jesus and the young church in the New Testament but we are introduced to Jesus the story teller. He tells wonderful stories about kings and beggars, about the rich and the poor, about the mad and the bad, about the haves and the have-nots. They are very similar to the stories that we hear today, your story and my story echo other stories from the past as well as the present and when we share these stories, when we talk with one another, *that* is when we meet each other and that, I believe, is often a moment when people feel valued and affirmed. For many this is a moment of healing. Stories then are vitally important.

Often part of the story deals with how we have coped with the news of the death of someone who has been close to us, perhaps someone we have loved, perhaps someone to whom we have been devoted. The period of bereavement will often follow a four stage process. Initially, and quite understandably, there is a period of shock which is often manifested physically. People will speak of having a dry throat and wanting to swallow and of feeling cold and even perspiring. Shock is followed by a period of depression and again this is a normal human response to grief. The depressive phase is not a clinical condition, requiring treatment, but rather a natural reaction which often follows an experience of loss. The third phase is one of withdrawal where the person needs to be alone and without interference from other people, however kindly meant. Again this is not a phenomenon that should give cause for concern but is part of the grieving process. It is a very important part because it provides a natural break from the past and an opportunity for the grieving person to acknowledge that death has occurred, that this had a profound effect upon them and they are confronted with a new situation.

The last part of the process is one of re-adjustment, when bereaved people begin to make adjustments within themselves and their lifestyle which indicate that they may have been able to incorporate the effect of what has happened and acknowledge the reality of the death. Not everyone will need to pass through all four of these stages, nor necessarily in the order in which I have described them.

The repeating of the story is an important element within the natural process of bereavement and it is a conversation repeated over and over again that offers the possibility of hope for the sufferer. The test for such a robust statement is to be found among those people who, for reasons beyond their control, have no story to tell. I remember well the situation a colleague once explained to me. Her family had grown up and one of her sons remained single and lived a very carefree life in which he would set out in his sailing boat often going across the channel to France and further afield into the Mediterranean to the North African coast and the Near East. He would moor his boat, work a while to earn money for food and then set off to his next destination. He would always drop a card home telling his parents where he was and where he expected to be next. One day he waved goodbye to his mother and set off on another voyage. Since he left she has received no postcard and no communication of his whereabouts and that was over twenty years ago. The conclusion that his parents naturally reached is that he is missing presumed dead. Now they have no story to tell and no fixed point. There is no body to identify and no hard evidence indicating death. The result is that they cannot begin to grieve, even though they know in their hearts that he is dead through one cause or another. It is in their words like living in suspended animation, or in a state of limbo.

This illustration demonstrates both the essential need for everyone to have a story to tell and also tangible evidence of the death of the person they grieve. It also places a responsibility upon those who communicate news of death (police, nursing staff, ministers et al) to ensure that they do so in a professional and caring way and that they ensure the person has enough basic information from which to develop their "story" at a later stage.

Anyone who has met or worked with a person suffering grief knows how much they desire to tell their story. What they seek is a listener, one with whom they can converse and, quite literally, bare their soul.

Whether you are the story teller at one moment or the listener at another, what is paramount is the meeting of two people in the telling of the story. I believe that listening to the story, often a heartrending story, of another person is a way of caring for them and valuing them. Telling the story is a way of helping with grief and I believe that "talking heals". What Christians believe is that God listens to our stories as well as bringing us into his story. Now his story is narrated for us on the human stage through the person of Jesus. This story tells us that Jesus met death with resurrection.

My hope is that this service is a means of help and support to all of you. My prayer is that today you have come near to God and been touched and strengthened by him, as you continue your own journey into a future yet to be revealed. I pray that on this journey you will be supported, encouraged and blessed by the presence of God and be guided, strengthened and renewed by his Holy Spirit.

Prayer

May those who are grieving always have a story to relate as a means of helping them come to terms with the death of the person they mourn. May your light shine into the darkest corners of their grief and give them hope where there is despair and inner peace where there is unrest and turbulence, Amen.

Remembrance

I was surprised. I was saddened and I have to say I was alarmed to hear it said about the Anniversary of the D Day Landings, "this will surely be the last anniversary because then there will be no one left to remember". Such comments are not only profoundly hurtful to those who do wish to remember which, from the sale of poppies alone, is more than 34 million people, but the comment also indicates a false and misguided understanding of memory. The sadness does not end here, because this is not just a comment about memory, but also about being human. Human beings are social; they are gregarious and they create and develop relationships between each other. Part of being human is to share and transfer memories, to pass on stories and traditions and to appreciate and understand our origins and history. Being human means being caught up in a narrative, playing on a stage with other people, and listening and learning from their experiences. Memories, quite definitely, do not die with the people who experience the event, but continue to live with others.

It is then vitally important to *remember*; today across the country people are gathering as others have in the past, and will do in the future, to remember those who have lost their lives in war. The only year a British service person has not been killed in active service since the end of WWII is 1968. Since 1945 well in excess of 120,000 British service personnel have been killed or injured in active service. There are 11 million veterans alive today who have served in the Armed Forces and associated organisations. More people have died in wars in the last Century than ever before in the history of mankind and, as a consequence, it is even more important to hold them in our memories. It was George Santayana, a Spanish born philosopher and critic who said in his 'Life of Reason' written in 1905 ......

'those who cannot remember the past are condemned to repeat it'. The same words are to be found at Dachau.

Remembering is at the heart of the Christian faith. It was at the Last Supper on the night before his arrest, that Jesus took bread and wine and told his disciples to do this in remembrance of him. They were to do it as an act of remembering. To this day, it is still a matter of debate whether Jesus was referring just to breaking the bread that was to become his body; or whether, more generally, he was asking them to remember all that he had said and done. So it is that every time Christians meet for the Communion service, they are caught up in an act of remembering, they are part of a narrative which is much bigger than themselves and they recognise the truth that remembering brings the past into the present to prepare them for the future—and the future is nothing less than life with God himself.

Reminiscence therapy has become de rigueur in mental health units for older people; especially those places which cater for older people with organic illnesses, like Alzheimer's, reminiscence therapy has proved to be both popular and useful. As the name suggests, the therapy provides an opportunity for people to recall their earlier life and to remember events from the past. Music, film and story are all used as vehicles to stimulate the memory process.

Memories are important for older people because they provide a context or what I have called a narrative. Because memory can provide a context it is *as* important for young people *as* it is for older people and yet in every generation, young people live for the present, the here and now, rather than the past, or even the future. Yet when important things happen to them, when there are life crises, when a close friend or relative dies, their memory banks open.

Counselling, psychotherapy and particularly psycho-analysis depend upon memory—upon a person's ability to recall events, experiences and feelings from the past. The problem is that our memory can be elusive which is well known to the therapist and the counsellor. They know that we prefer to stay with and retain the good memories and subjugate and repress the difficult and painful memories. This is understandable, as well as being human; and, of course, healthy repression allows us to block out those memories which hurt us and stultify our growth. This surely must be the reason why people known to us who have spent time in prisoner of war camps or worse concentration camps, very rarely, if ever, talk about their experiences.

I remember well a man in his 70s in the last parish in which I worked coming to the 50th anniversary service we arranged for VJ Day. The Norfolk's were among the first to be captured when they landed in Singapore. He had been a prisoner of war of the Japanese in Burma. He had suffered himself and had appalling memories of what had happened to him and those around him and he had survived. He thanked me profusely for the service of remembrance because, he said, it was the first opportunity in 50 years that he had had to visit those memories. He reminded me that when he and his fellow prisoners of war returned to this country, VE Day had come and gone and he was but one person in the forgotten army. Even if he had wanted to recall the memories and tell the story, he realised there was no point because the world had moved on and Burma, the Japanese and the Atom Bomb were no longer on people's agendas. It really is very difficult to tell your story when nobody wants to listen. It is also very difficult, as time goes by, to recall and relive painful and hurtful memories.

Nevertheless more people today go to counsellors and therapists than ever before and many of the people who returned from the camps set up in the Second World War and more recently those who have been caught up in the Killing Fields of Cambodia, who were subjected to ethnic cleansing in Bosnia, who experienced the overthrow of Iraq, who are suffering enormous tragedies in Syria and continuing terrorist attacks today have benefited from counselling and therapy. The skilled therapist is able to help people overcome their reticence, reserve and sometimes fear of painful memories so that they are able to tell their story, to recall what happened to them and to reminisce.

Remembering provides us with a context, a sense of history, a way of coming to terms with the dark areas of our past, and the material for our personal story. Remembering past experiences and people we have known is not something which happens once a year at the Cenotaph in London, at the war memorial here or when flowers are placed on the graves of loved ones. Remembering is something we all do all the time. It is dynamic and it is done in order to help us re-enact the past in the present in preparation for the future.

I began with the comment—"Surely this will be the last anniversary of the D Day Landings because there will no one left to remember"—not only is this comment hurtful and erroneous, but it also demonstrates a lack of understanding about the nature of God. God exists beyond our imaginings, outside time and space and there are elements of God unknown to us. We describe this as the mystery of God to which we are drawn in our meditations, prayers and worship. Even if there were to be just one person who is not remembered by any human being and never has been, that person would still be stored in God's divine memory. That person like everyone else is remembered by God simply because every human being is precious in the sight of God. Unlike our memories, God's memory does not need to depend upon particular times or anniversaries, place names or events in order to be recalled. Just as a thousand years are like a day in God's economy, so his memory is constantly alive and always available. Let us then commit our memories to the divine memory where God recalls all who have gone before us and blesses them. It is now in the presence of God that we join a far greater narrative where remembering gives us nourishment, gives us strength and hope to live with the past, celebrate the present and step into the future with faith and courage.

Prayer

Let us pray that we will always be ready to remember to avoid repeating the past. May our memories enable us to re-enact the past in the present, in order to prepare us for the future. Good Lord, help us, we pray, to be ready to listen to the stories of others and support them in their need, Amen.

The Need for Light

Without exception at this time of the year every year the incidence of depression rises quite dramatically. In fact, there is a condition known as SAD—Seasonal Affective Disorder. The reason why the numbers of people suffering from depression increases is because there is less light at this time of the year. As you know, the shortest day is on 21 December which, in 2014, marked the 45th anniversary of my ordination as a priest. Though starved of light 45 years ago in Worcester Cathedral, I recollect that it was a very happy occasion and not in any way depressing. To my surprise I was given many gifts and the most intriguing was from Melanie—an electric drill!

I suppose you could say that those people who live near the Arctic Circle look forward to a winter of depression because they experience darkness 24 hours a day. On the other hand, in the summer they enjoy 24 hours of light each day. What is indisputable is that lack of light increases depression.

One of the main themes running through the Christian faith is the theme of light which begins today—Advent Sunday. Advent Sunday marks the beginning of the penitential season of preparation for Christmas. It also sees the beginning of the new liturgical year. Today the calendar of prayers and readings, of festivals and holy days begins again. From Advent Sunday for the next three months up to the Festival of Candlemas the emphasis will be on light and heralding Jesus as the light of the world. Today we light the first candle of the five which make up the Advent Ring. In fact the light theme occurs again on Easter Eve and I will come back to that in a moment.

In the Chapel of Keble College in Oxford is a painting of Jesus standing by a gate holding a lantern. 'Lux Mundi'—a title for Christ derived from St John's Gospel Chapter 6 Verse 12. It is the subject of Holman Hunt's famous picture (of which the artist painted two copies), the other is at St Paul's Cathedral. Oxford is a place I know well, as is Keble College, because I went to school in Oxford.

The painting is called 'The Light of the World'. It describes the theme of light identifying Jesus as the light of the world through whom shines the love of God. One way in which the Church represents this is by the use of candles. At baptismal services candles are often given to the candidates to remind them that they have joined a community of light. On the second of February—Candlemas—there are many churches where processions of candles celebrate God's light shining in the person of his son Jesus. It was old Simeon, you remember, who waited patiently with the ageing Anna for the arrival of this particular child. He identified him immediately and, in St Luke's Gospel, he speaks the words of the Nunc Dimittis with the line 'a light to lighten the Gentiles, and the glory of thy people Israel'. These words, in turn, pick up the theme of one of the favourite Old Testament readings used at carol services over Christmas …. 'the people who dwell in darkness have seen great light': and then again it was the light of a star which led the Wise Men to David's City, Bethlehem, to see this young child that everyone was talking about.

There are special ceremonies in the Church on Easter Eve, when a new fire is lit from which the great Easter Candle takes its light. A candle is borne by one of the ministers through the church from the main door to the high altar. The minister stops three times and either sings or speaks the words 'Christ our light', to which all reply 'thanks be to God'. The Easter or Paschal Candle symbolizes the presence of Christ as the light of the world and is lit throughout the year at successive services. From the Easter Candle the smaller candles for the newly baptized are lit, linking them to Christ the light to whom they have just committed their lives. A threefold statement of faith is made when the candidates declare that they turn to Christ and repent of their sins.

The question which arises is why light is so important. It is important because:

- It banishes darkness.
- It provides clarity.
- It offers hope.
- It is an antidote to depression.
- It is the stuff of glory.

You will hear people say that it is important that some light is thrown on the situation. In the age in which we live there is an enormous need for light. Whether we are talking about the darkness of depression and the nightmares of mental illness, or the dullness and isolation of increasingly privatized lives— where now 40% of all housing is occupied by one person or whether we are talking about finding a way through the plethora of spin which tumbles all too easily from the mouths of our politicians, or whether we are thinking of the blackness and the bleakness of terrorism and the continuing bombing in Iraq and Syria, or whether it is that frightening darkness of simply not knowing, becoming lost and feeling abandoned, the darkness of grief and bereavement, and so many other situations which can be dark and frightening—our prayer is for light to be poured into these situations. We herald Christ as the light of the world because he illuminates the journey to God. His light reveals our shortcomings, his light shines in the dark corners of our souls and his light brings the promise of glory. Celebrate Advent, celebrate Christmas, celebrate Candlemas, celebrate Easter and the Paschal Candle, and celebrate Pentecost and the gift of God's Holy Spirit. When you have done this, you will have truly celebrated and worshipped God.

Prayer

Give us light, we pray, to shine in the dark places of our minds and to banish darkness in people's lives. May the light of Christ illuminate the church with love and bring solace to the those who live in the darkness of terror, violence and cruelty, Amen.

Christmas

It is now commonplace to say that the 11th September changed the world. It is true—it did change the world, because international terrorism reached unimagined new depths, not least because all the victims were civilians.

Human history is littered with episodes of war and destruction but never has the world been in greater need of peace than in our own time. The fact that peacekeeping forces are stretched to the limit is evidence enough of the number of places where peace is a fragile commodity. This is worrying enough but when you add to it the techniques of modern warfare which, in the wrong hands, can create devastation, it is little wonder that people feel uncertain, confused, anxious, and sometimes very frightened.

Both in the Jewish and in the Christian faiths there is a prayer for the peace of Jerusalem. Three world religions lay claim to Jerusalem—Christianity, Judaism and Islam. Never has there been a moment when that prayer is more needed, more urgent, more necessary. Jerusalem has always been a major influence in the world and peace in Jerusalem is a metaphor for peace in the world. When Jerusalem is at peace with itself and its neighbours, the peace spills over into the wider world. Today, there is a need for peace in Jerusalem so that Israel and Palestine can live alongside each other. Establishing peace in Jerusalem may help to bring peace to the Middle East and further afield. Let us, like those who have gone before us, continue to pray for peace to be established in Jerusalem.

One of the Lessons in the traditional service of Nine Lessons and Carols is from Isaiah, Ch. 9, where there is the reference to Wonderful Counsellor, Mighty God, Everlasting Father, Prince of Peace. At the centre of the Christian faith is the person and the personality of Jesus who was given the title "Prince of Peace". The Christian Gospel which is preached today has not changed throughout the ages. At the heart of this Gospel is the great truth of Christmas, that God became man. In today's jargon we might say Christmas is the celebration of God "downloading" himself. That God walked among us in the person of Jesus is not only central to the Christian faith and one of its great truths, it is also the Gospel that we need to continue to preach if justice and peace are to have a chance of being established in the world we inhabit. We somehow have to find an end to hatred and violence so that peace can truly come to reign in Jerusalem and throughout the rest of the world.

As you prepare to celebrate Christmas, I hope with friends and family, please remember to pray for peace in the world. If you have an opportunity to come and gaze into the crib and look at the tiny baby, remember the great truth of Christmas, that God was "down loaded". What this means is that when you look into the face of the baby, you are looking into the face of God himself.

Pray for peace, be at peace with yourself and those around you and offer this peace to those you meet now and in the days to come. Share with me the vision that was given to us, not in the New Testament, but in the Old Testament. Again, we delve into Isaiah where we find these words ...

"The wolf will live with the lamb,
the leopard will lie down with the goat,
the calf and the lion and the yearling together; and the little child will lead them.
The cow will feed with the bear,
their young will lie down together,
and the lion will eat straw like the ox.
The infant will play near the hole of the cobra,
and the young child will put his hand into the viper's nest.
They will neither harm nor destroy

on all my holy mountain,
that the earth will be full of the knowledge of the Lord, as the
waters cover the sea."

Here is a vision of peace. Here, is a picture of animals feeding together, of violent animals being led by a little child, of peace on the Holy Mountain, of the earth being full of the knowledge of God and a world, at last, at peace with itself. This is our prayer. May you and those around you have a happy, holy and peaceful Christmas.

Prayer

At Christmas time we are aware of how important it is to work and pray for peace. We pray, O Lord, that the peace of the Christ child will become established in those places where there is terror, violence and war. We pray especially for all world leaders who are committed to promoting peace and justice in our world, Amen.

Christmastime

It was a rather cold November afternoon when Melanie and I visited Bentalls in Kingston-upon-Thames. This has been a favourite shopping centre for Melanie ever since she was at school at Ashtead in Surrey. Now it was time for more retail therapy and what better place. What struck me was that not a single Christmas card illustrated the story of the birth of Jesus.

Christmas has become so very secularized and Christ has been all but removed from it. Our task, as Christians, is to do all we can to put Christ and the Christian story back into Christmas and encourage others to celebrate the mighty truth that God became man in Palestine and, as John Betjeman says, lives today in bread and wine.

We do need to be clear about our Christian faith, about what we believe and distinctions do need to be made because, otherwise, edges can become so easily blurred and Jesus becomes muddled up with Father Christmas, the vicar with God and Father Christmas with the vicar—after all both of them wear long robes!

You may have heard that, after Christmas one year, the vicar was hunting for the figure of the Christ Child which seemed to have gone missing from the crib. As he searched, he saw a little girl pushing a pram up the aisle of the church and stopped by the crib. Very gently and carefully she returned the figure of the baby Jesus to the crib and said "there you are, I told you that if you gave me a pram I would make sure that you were the first person to have a ride in it!"

The East window of the Lady Chapel in Shipdham shows the Christmas scene in all its fullness. There is the crib scene with the Holy family, the animals, the shepherds, and the three kings all gathered together. Above the stable are two of the seven archangels, Michael and Raphael and above them reaching into the apex of the arch are twelve angels playing harps, lyres, zithers, and cymbals. Above them is the hand of God pointing to the new born saviour of the world. Here in all its fullness is the Christmas story.

In Norwich Cathedral there is a truly wonderful series of bosses stretching the length of the choir and nave. One favourite is Noah's Ark. Nevertheless, I am always captivated by the Christmas boss where the young baby is indisputably a little girl—the hips are the give away!

It can be a very confusing world and a world where it is not easy to be a Christian. So, hold fast to your faith, be firmly rooted in the love of God, be confident in communicating the Christmas message, be imaginative in the way that you talk about the things of God, and never stop being courageous and full of hope that the glory of God will shine in the dark places of the earth and that Christ will be put back into Christmas. After the census results, it seems the task is going to be particularly difficult in Norwich where 43% claim to have no religion!

Something visible and tangible like the Christmas crib, a stained glass window or a boss in the roof of Norwich cathedral and, which I believe to be an asset, are our church buildings. Our church buildings are crucial visual aids marking the presence of Christianity in every community in the land. We need always to cherish them and ensure that they are adapted to meet the needs of the local community

Let me finish with these words written especially for Christmas...

When the song of the angels is stilled,
When the star in the sky is gone,
When the kings and the princes are home,
When the shepherds are back with their flocks,
The work of Christmas begins:

To find the lost,
To heal the broken,
To feed the hungry,
To release the prisoner,
To rebuild the nation,
To bring peace among people,
To make music in the heart, Amen.

Prayer

O God Almighty, Lord Divine we pray that your Son, Jesus Christ, may forever be central to Christmas so that those who come to the stable can gaze upon his infant face and see there your glory. Thank you for coming into the world to share our humanity so that we can share in your divinity, Amen.

Learning Disabilities

The Christmas season runs from Advent to Candlemas—over 2 months. Just three days after the great festival, the celebration continues of that amazing truth that God became man in Palestine and, as Betjeman says, lives today in bread and wine.

I had the privilege, when I was in Lincolnshire, of attending the introduction of the Bishop of Lincoln to the House of Lords. It was grand occasion following a handsome lunch in the Lords' restaurant. One of the first things a noble prelate (as they are called) has to do is give their maiden speech. The Bishop of Lincoln has now done this and he concentrated on the whole question of immigration, not least because Lincolnshire, especially in the South, is a magnet for migrant workers. They work in the fields harvesting vegetables and often doing work nobody else will do. As you may imagine he expounded on the incarnation—the truth of Christmas. I had already warned him that a maiden speech is by convention non controversial and that he, being the Christian he is, would find that difficult!! Then he chose to talk about Jesus sharing our humanity which is always controversial because it speaks about the human condition.

It is little wonder that the church needs 2 months to celebrate the truth of Christmas extending, as it does, to include Epiphany and the huge insight that Jesus is a universal figure. He is there for everyone whoever they are and wherever they come from. It is a truth that the farmers of South Lincolnshire are having to learn.

For all this talk about the celebration of Christmas, never forget that the way the church arranges its calendar means that we have already celebrated 3 festivals since Christmas. Boxing day is the feast day of the first deacon and martyr St Stephen. The following day is the remembrance of St John the Divine and then the feast day of the Holy Innocents follows. Celebrating

Red Letter days (which today have a different meaning—a drive in a racing car or steam engine for example) continues during seasonal periods like Christmas and Easter. The Holy Innocents were all the little boys whom King Herod decreed should be killed in his search for the child Jesus. He had heard from the 3 Wise Men that a new King had been born and he was worried about the possible threat to his own position. In those days the remedy for any threat was the extinction of the people who posed the threat.

Forty years of my own ministry has involved working in the field of mental health which includes people with Learning Disabilities. For me today's Holy Innocents are people with Learning Disabilities, especially children. It was only just over 100 hundred years ago (1902) that the distinction was made in law between mental health and learning disability. The language has changed beyond recognition. In those days a person with a mental health problem was called a lunatic and those with a learning disability a cretin or idiot. Later this was to change to subnormality and to my astonishment I heard someone use the expression very recently.

Today people with Learning Disabilities are provided with social care in the community. There are very few beds left in hospitals. In the Mental Health Trust for which I worked there are just 12 beds altogether and these are essentially for respite purposes. Gone are the days of the large isolated hospitals for the mentally handicapped. Most of them have become executive housing estates.

The Disability Discrimination Act is a challenge to any Christian Community and, as your Archdeacon will remind you, it includes people with mental health problems and learning disabilities. I well recall attending a church, let me say, South of London. It was a large evangelical church. Before the main service began, a group of some 20-30 adults with learning disabilities arrived with their carers. I was delighted until they were all shepherded into a specially prepared area at the back of the church. This, I thought, is not what the DDA had in mind. Oh, that they could have been naturally integrated into the congregation and perhaps even encouraged to take part in the service. Why, for example, could they not be sidespeople? There is certainly a challenge in the DDA for all of us. How do we plan for full integration in the life and worship of the church and its community?

I was sad to discover that there was no-one with a disability in the top ten nominated for sports personality of the year, even though in the para Olympics we won 102 medals, 42 of which were gold and were second only to the host nation, China. The compensation was that Eleanor Simmonds won young sports personality of the year for her amazing success in the swimming pool.

The role of the church is to be Jesus to anyone with a disability and this means hard work and courage. Of course we have to pioneer new ways of integration and inclusion, means of support and a readiness to educate the local community and learn lessons from those already ahead of us. Additionally we have a responsibility to promote the needs of people with learning disabilities and this is not easy. As is often said there are no votes in this particular venture. If we were talking about an animal charity, then convincing people of the needs would not be a problem. There is an example of this from New York city. A blind man and his dog were injured after being hit by a van and both needed hospital treatment. Soon the flowers began to arrive and it was noted that they were all addressed to the dog!!

Here at St Matthew's you already have a highly developed sense of community service and I am simply seeking to enlarge that. Being of service to those in need derives from our belief in the incarnation and incarnation is always controversial. May God bless all your endeavours undertaken in His name and may you continue to enjoy and celebrate Christmas and its great of God at work in our world, Amen.

A Just War

Each year a weekend is identified to celebrate Armed Forces day and Veterans day. Melanie and I were privileged to be part of a cruise to celebrate the 70th. Anniversary of the Dunkirk evacuation. I was the chaplain for the week which was frenetic, memorable and deeply charged emotionally. From Sunday to Thursday we visited War Grave cemeteries at Dunkirk, Arnhem, Ypres, the Somme, and the D day landing beaches where wreaths were laid at the memorial monuments. The endless rows of white headstones in beautifully tended grounds were a poignant reminder of the futility, sorrow, waste, and sheer destruction of war. On July 1st.1916 on the first day of the battle of the Somme 20,000 British troops were killed, the largest number on any one day in the history of this country. As well as the monuments to the unknown soldier, there were thousands of memorials to unknown soldiers, sailors and airmen with the words 'Known unto God'. Most encouraging were the large numbers of school children who were visiting the sites and laying wreaths. Ypres itself has been rebuilt and become a centre for peace and reconciliation. Here, at the Menin Gate Memorial, every night of the year including Christmas day at 8pm the gate is shut and the Last Post sounded. There is rarely ever less than 100 people and often more than a thousand.

Let me then for a moment speak about war and particularly the principles of a just war.

One of the paradoxes of the human spirit is that just as soon as a war begins, people look forward to more peaceful times and begin to wonder just how much they will have to endure before a lasting peace is established. What prompted them to go to war in the first place also has to do with the human spirit. Usually wars begin over disputes about national identity or national boundaries. Just as each individual needs to have an identity and clearly defined boundaries, so do societies and nations. Threaten to do away with a nation's identity, or annex it to another country or ignore its roots, traditions and history and there will be a price to pay. This is because nations, like individual human beings, need to know who they are, where they have come from and the general direction in which they are going, if they are to function adequately. Any external threat to national identity and national boundaries always leads to confusion and disagreement and sometimes inevitably to war.

Once war has been declared there is an accepted code of practice which most civilized countries accept, governing the conduct of the war. Of course adherence to such a code is voluntary and perhaps it is most clearly seen in the aftermath of war when certain combatants are charged with war crimes. The code of practice is what is often referred to as the principles of a *just war* which were first developed not by a politician, or lawgiver but a theologian. The Church has always acknowledged that there are some situations, albeit very few, when a nation is justified in taking up arms and engaging in war. These principles are clearly defined and are as follows:

• The decision by a country to go to war should be a last resort.

Everything else that is available should have been tried and shown to have failed before taking the ultimate step. To have to take that step can understandably be seen as a sign of failure, because all other efforts have been unsuccessful. It was Archbishop Runcie who preached the sermon in St Paul's Cathedral at the end of the Falklands war and he was not popular for saying that resorting to war is a sign of failure. What others wanted was a message of congratulation for the victory that had been won and this carries the overtones of triumphalism which clearly has no part in the Christian Gospel.

- The second principle is one of self defence.

That is to say that a country should only wage war in order to defend itself. This principle was clearly demonstrated in the Gulf war when Kuwait sought to defend its own borders and by doing so to continue to preserve its identity as a small nation state.

- The third principle relates to the weaponry which is being used.

The weaponry should be directed towards the ending of the war as quickly as possible and establishing a lasting peace. This means, of course, that every effort should be made to ensure that weaponry is not being stockpiled and escalated. The arena of war is no place for hype.

- Allied to this principle is that which indicates that only enough weapons should be employed to achieve a particular purpose.

If the objective is to render inoperable the railway station then the nearby town is not bombed as well. It was just this principle in the just war theory that led people to criticise the bombing of Dresden which was seen as saturation bombing motivated by the need to retaliate. In this country places like Coventry were indiscriminately bombed. The Gulf war on the other hand is a good example of the way in which very sophisticated weaponry was used by the Allies to achieve particular targets and then, when this was done, to withdraw.

- The mention of the need to retaliate brings us to another aspect of the principles which is to avoid retaliation.

Retaliation carries echoes of phrases like 'an eye for an eye and a tooth for a tooth'. Again there is no place for such sentiment in the Christian Gospel and Jesus was unequivocal when he said 'You have learned that they were told, eye for eye, tooth for tooth. But what I tell you is this: 'do not set yourself against the man who wrongs you;' and again 'you have learned that they were told, love your neighbours, hate your enemies. But what I tell you is this: love your enemies and pray for your persecutors; only so can you be children of your Heavenly Father who makes his sun rise on good and bad alike and sends the rain on the honest and the dishonest. If you love only those who love you, what reward can you expect?'

- The last element which derives from the principles of a just war is a concern to protect the innocent.

Every effort should be made to ensure that people who are not part of the activity of war should be protected. We know only too well of the tens of thousands of civilians who lost their lives in the second world war and this indeed is one of the major differences between that war and the Great War (1914-18). Nor can it be said that the situation has improved since the second world war; we only need to reflect on contemporary warfare to realise that the situation has become much worse. In Syria and Iraq car bombs lead to indiscriminate killing and people losing their livelihoods, their homes and families.

Where whole communities have been wiped out like Cambodia and Liberia it is called ethnic cleansing—a euphemism for slaughter and destruction. If just war principles had been in place, there might have been less horror stories coming out of these countries.

It soon becomes very clear that if all these principles were acted upon by any nation or group of people that contemplated war, wars would be less likely to begin.

However, in the real world we have to live with human frailty, hatred, greed, and selfishness, and what amounts to a total disregard for any concept of a just war. Once again this means that the cry goes up when wars begin 'let us establish peace just as soon as possible'. However, these principles do help with the preservation of peace. Far better to try to keep the peace before going to war, than to search for an elusive peace once war has been declared. If we were to take just one of the principles that we have been considering, for example, only going to war as a last resort, this in itself would help to preserve peace and sustain some sort of equanimity, if only those involved appreciated the value of what Winston Churchill once described as 'jaw jaw, rather than war war'. Once war has been declared, in its wake quickly follow the horrors of war—the loss of human life, the enormous suffering and pain imposed upon people, the devastation of the countryside, towns and villages, the destruction of commercial, industrial and educational life, and the enormous financial burden resulting from expenditure on weapons of destruction which everyone knows could be put to far better use for the good of all people.

The peace that Jesus speaks of is, he says, not of this world. It is a lasting peace, an eternal peace and a peace which is initiated by God himself. It is a divine peace expressed and experienced in the affairs of human beings. There are many aspects to divine peace and the one which is attractive is the peace which. 'passes all understanding'. This peace lasts and lasts and it is not subject to the whims and changes of everyday life, nor does it rely on human frailty, but like a good book or a good piece of music it goes on. Furthermore you can return to it and relish the fact that it is still there.

This is the sort of peace which is at the very heart of God himself. Here is the promise of eternity and the hope of things yet unknown which take us beyond our imaginings and the limited horizons of this world. Here surely is an antidote to the violence that Martin Luther King spoke of when he said 'The ultimate weakness of violence is that it is a descending spiral, begetting the very thing it seeks to destroy; returning violence for violence multiplies violence adding deeper darkness to a night already devoid of stars. Darkness cannot drive out darkness; only light can do that. Hate cannot drive out hate; only love can do that and I believe that that love is the love which comes from God Himself.'

As it says in the camp at Dachau 'those who cannot remember the past, are condemned to repeat it'

Prayer

We pray that the world may enjoy peace and justice and that the leaders of the nations may strive to achieve this end. When war is declared, we ask that the principles of the 'Just War' will be implemented and possible excesses contained, so that people caught up in the conflict, can have hope. Good Lord, we pray, keep our vision alive, Amen.

Mountains

Mountains have always had an aura of mystery, not least because so often their peaks are shrouded in mist. We read in Chapter 19 in the Book of Exodus … 'Moses brought the people out from the camp to meet God, and they took their stand at the foot of the mountain. Mount Sinai was all smoking because the Lord had come down upon it in fire; the smoke went up like the smoke of a kiln; all the people were terrified, and the sound of the trumpet grew ever louder. Whenever Moses spoke, God answered him in a peal of Thunder'.

There are at least 36 mountains mentioned in the Bible and some more than others are identified as places of holiness, places where the mystery of God can be touched and places where the divine presence enshrouds the people of God. Have no fear, it is not my intention to talk about all 36 but rather to select a few which play a significant part in the saving activity of God.

One of the privileges I enjoy is the opportunity from time to time to lecture on cruises. Melanie and I have been able to visit the Baltic when St Petersburg celebrated its tri centenary. I take with me my notes and power point presentations about Gothic and Romanesque architecture particularly; but I also talk about medieval sculpture and one lecture is devoted to telling the Christian story illustrated in the sculpture especially that found on the capitals. One of my favourites is in the Cathedral of Gerona and it shows Noah's Ark. It is no larger than a dessert plate, yet manages to convey the story of the Ark through the artist's attention to detail.

After consuming knowledge by eating the forbidden fruit, Adam and Eve discovered and developed the human facility for making choices. As we know from the way in which the saga unfolds, the people became so rebellious that the Lord decided to take action and have a clean sweep concentrating his attention on all the creatures gathered in the Ark. It was the first intimation of a theology of the remnant which was to become so important when the people of God were exiled to Babylon. Noah leaves the Ark when it comes to rest on the top of Mount Ararat.

It was to Mount Sinai that Moses was called to receive from God the legislative blueprint on which both the history and religion of the Jewish people were established. Here in the misty vapour Moses met God and received the Ten Commandments. These foundation laws were the basis of the Roman Empire and later our own legal system, which protects property, lives and family life.

In successive books of the Old Testament these primary laws were to be expanded into the Book of the Law. The symbolism of the Ark is continued because it is the Ark in which the Commandments are kept. Their final resting place is to be the Temple in Jerusalem.

Jerusalem, the City of God is built on Mount Zion, which is the south-west hill of Jerusalem, the older and higher part of the city. Jerusalem becomes fully established as the City of David and the City of God in the reign of King Solomon and has remained so until this day. Although there have been many vicissitudes and any number of occasions when the Jewish nation has been exiled and dispersed across the world, nevertheless Jerusalem takes pride of place in the Jewish psyche. It is also a focal point for the Christian and Moslem religions and the three have co-existed for hundreds of years. At the moment there is an uneasy tension and it is a moot point whether tension is intrinsic to the life of this city.

It was in Jerusalem that the events of Holy Week took place. Before then Jesus had taken Peter, James and John to another mountain. It is what you might call the 'mountain of change'. It was here that Jesus was transfigured. It was here that this trinity of apostles experienced something of the mystery of God and the divinity of Christ. It is an experience which could not have failed to change them. We too pray that we might experience transfiguration and pursue a pilgrimage of change so that we might, in the words of the hymn, 'change from glory to glory'. Outside Jerusalem is the Mount of Olives. Jesus had washed his disciples' feet, eaten the last supper with them, been betrayed, and given us the Eucharist before he and the eleven made their way to the Mount of Olives. From here he moves to Gethsemane—a place of anguish and identity—to betrayal and arrest. It is on a hill outside the city walls where he dies on a cross, a death which was a turning point in the affairs of the world and in the saving activity of God. It was on the Mount of Olives that Jesus departed from the eleven. His final act was to bless them and commission them for their own ministry as he blesses and commissions you and me today. We are charged with being his body in the world, being his hands, his eyes, and feet. Let it be part of our prayer that generations of people will climb Steep Hill in Lincoln and find in this cathedral holiness, mystery, tranquillity, the peace of God, and the resources for their own pilgrimage and ministry in the world.

Prayer

Lord God, we come to see your presence in many different ways including the natural environment. We pray that we may appreciate your mystery in the wonders of nature. We pray too that we may be encouraged to look upwards and outwards as we scale the mountainous journey to our eternal home and your abiding glory, Amen.

People with Hearing Difficulties

Jesus was one of the best story tellers in the world and this afternoon at this special service I want to follow his example and tell you two stories. I also want to use some of the material from today's service as building blocks for my stories. The reference to Bishop Grosseteste of Lincoln included a thought about buildings. The buildings reminded me of a story that I was asked to tell with a group of people on a group dynamics course; it had to include a building, a river and a mountain. The mention of St Hugh's swan reminded me about the way I began. My story started with a bird and you can make the bird represent whatever you like. It can be anything you would like to make it. My own bird is any one of that group of five people with learning disabilities who visited a zoo in the Isle of Wight and were asked to leave because they might frighten the animals!!

Here then is my first story. Once upon a time high on a mountain on the continent of Europe snuggling under an overhanging rock was a bird's nest. If you could have moved very close to the nest, you would have seen cracks appearing in the shell of one of the eggs. A few hours later after a lot of tapping a beak broke through the shell and for the first time the tiny bird breathed in air. It was not long before the shell cracked open and the baby bird was drying off in the sun. Its mother immediately started the feeding the first of the little birds that had hatched in her nest. Soon the baby bird was sitting up and spreading its wings ready to fly away from the mountain. With an ample diet of juicy worms, the baby bird grew strong quickly. Being the first born, it was the first to leave the nest. The little bird said "goodbye" to its mother and flew away from under the rock near the top of the mountain. Soon the rocks on the mountainside gave way to gorse and grass and small bushes. Ahead of it the little bird saw the outline of a belt of trees. Instinctively, it knew it would find water in the trees. It settled on a branch low on a tree and there beneath it was a tiny stream. Very gingerly the little bird moved close to the edge of the stream in order to drink the water.

Refreshed, it flew on, following the course of the stream which soon grew into a river which ran swiftly away from the base of the mountain, down a valley where sheep were grazing. Even though the trees had given way to fields and you would expect it to be much lighter, it became darker and darker and this is because it was night time. As so often happens in this part of the world when night time comes, especially early in the year, the temperature drops and it starts to become very cold. The little bird which had been born in the mountains, followed the course of the river and the fields gave way to the outskirts of a large village. Here, there were lots of buildings and some of them were lit up on the inside. Sometimes the light was quite dim because it was created by a fire flickering in the grate and sometimes it was bright because the lights had been switched on.

By this time the little bird was becoming cold and hungry. It was a long time since it had left its home and mother high up on the mountain and so it settled on a window sill of one of the houses and looked in through the window. It saw creatures with two legs like itself but with arms instead of wings. These creatures were called human beings. They looked to be enjoying themselves and the little bird could hear the music that they were dancing to. At this moment the wind blew and ruffled up the feathers on the little bird's body and it felt a shiver go right through it. One of the humans saw this and drew the attention of the other human beings to the little bird. They stopped dancing and moved over to the window. They shouted and started banging on the window and waving their arms around. This frightened the little bird and it flew away and, since that day, no-one has ever seen it again.

And now to my second story which is a much shorter one. The third saint mentioned in our service today was the very well known Bishop of Lincoln, Edward King. The little boy that featured in the account of Bishop King reminded me of the second story which concerned a small boy whom I am going to call James.

I was a student at the time working during my vacation in a hospital for people with learning disabilities just outside St Albans. On this particular day, I was seconded to the children's ward and asked to help care for James. James was eight years old and very severely disabled. He had to be turned over by a member of staff because he was not able to do this himself. He was unable to see or to hear and his waking day was spent lying in what can be best described as a hammock. Nevertheless, it was possible to have a tiny bit of communication with him and, if you tickled his toes, a huge smile would spread across his face. Before James reached the age of nine he had died. This had been anticipated by those responsible for his care in the light of his very severe disabilities. What his short life was able to achieve was to bring out some very specific and special qualities in other people, particularly those with responsibility for his day to day care. James was so disabled that he could not make a direct contribution to those around him. Rather his disability brought out a response in others on whom he depended to care for him and provide for his basic needs. Central to the Christian faith is the belief that we are made in the image of God. That image can take many forms and in James the image reminds us of the vulnerability of God. This vulnerability we glimpse in the person of Jesus Christ through whom God was revealed to us.

The story of James reminds us that a world without disability would be a much poorer world. This same world needs to hear these stories. Increasingly, the world is becoming deaf to the stories we hear in the Bible and particularly the Christian story. A deaf world needs all of you to help it to hear these stories. You are the building blocks of the church and you have a critical art to play in helping a deaf world to hear. Just as you have to develop other faculties to compensate for your deafness so too does the world. If it refuses to hear, it needs you to teach it other ways to understand. This communication is vital if the glory of God is going to be revealed in the world in which we live.

Prayer

There are many people whose lives are restricted by deafness and disability and we ask simply that there will always be a place of honour for them in society. May the deaf help the world to hear the cries of those who are victims of prejudice, bigotry and ignorance. Please, we pray, infuse them with your Spirit so that they can learn to hear in other ways your call to be vehicles of love in the world, Amen.

Prison Chaplains

The title of your conference "Here I am" are the words that the prophet Isaiah uses in response to his vision of God in the temple. It is this reading which provides the Old Testament lesson at an ordination service and so immediately directs us to the heart of our ministry as priests and deacons and prophets. Isaiah gives us an account of the experience through which he received his call to the prophetic office. Aware of his own shortcomings and weaknesses when he sees God in glory face to face, he is filled with terror. One of the Seraphs flies towards him and touches his lips with a hot coal taken from the altar. This purges and cleanses him so that he can stand in the divine presence without fear. His response to God's call in the sixth chapter of Isaiah is to say "Here am I; send me". Like you and me he is authorised for ministry. In his case he is to speak again and again a word which will be heard but never understood. Indeed the only effect of his preaching will be to stultify his hearers and render hearing impossible. He asks how long this is to go on and receives the depressing answer "until the end". Ah, I see you have made the connection. It is not difficult to identify with this man of God. There is hope because in the Isaiahanic tradition there is the suggestion of a remnant which will take forward the word of God. In the meantime, Isaiah began his ministry fully aware that, certainly in the short term, he would fail.

"Here I am"—I is an Anglican priest licensed to be a chaplain in Her Majesty's Prison Service. At the core of the Anglican tradition is the Trinitarian formula of revelation, tradition and reason and, like the trinity itself, these three core principles need to held in balance. If we take a fairly simple issue like the ordination of women as bishops, we quickly discover that the arguments and reasonings range from the Scylla of ecclesiology to the Charybdis of headship. Apply some reason and the debate, if debate it is, should have been had when women were ordained as deacons into the sacred ministry. There is now no reason why they should not proceed to the episcopate. There may well be feelings and feelings are, of course, the driving force in decision making in contemporary society. Cogito ergo sum, the Cartesian tag has been replaced by sensio ergo sum or some would say Tesco ergo sum!

Stay with this Trinitarian framework for your own ministry in the prison service. It is not unlike the threefold ministry of hospital chaplains. Hospital chaplains and prison chaplains do not only share a care for the mentally ill in common but also exercise their ministry within a similar framework. Your threefold ministry is to the prisoners, the staff and the organisation as a whole. I will leave you to decide how the ministry of Father, Son and Holy Spirit applies to these three areas of prison life.

Because the Anglican tradition is so wide-ranging and comprehensive it does embrace within itself a place for the liberal, a place to test new ideas. The last time Bill and I heard your Bishop speaking at the Mission and Public Affairs Council of the General Synod, he was on good form doing what he does best which is to shake up our grey cells. The church is embarrassed about punishment, he said, and so punishment is left to the ungodly. Part of your work as chaplains is to remind the institution that God can act in a way which is not a way in which humans act. Isaiah found this out when he was called to ministry.

Before Peter Selby was Bishop for Prisons, the Bishop was the one who appointed me as his Archdeacon, Bob Hardy. Bob told me how confused he was when the first pagan chaplain was appointed in the prison service. He loved the work and he valued the chaplains and he spent many hours in prisons throughout the country. This work was recognised when he was awarded a

CBE. Well, we have moved on since Bob was Bishop for Prisons. You work in a multi-faith and multi-cultural society where the buzz word is spirituality. Some call this world post-modern. I call it neo-romantic and nowadays everything from quartz crystals to aromatherapy and from humanism to Islam is all contained within the one word spirituality. The challenge is to develop and define a spirituality which is Christian and rooted in the Anglican tradition. At the same time, the spirituality we promote has to be able to engage with those of other faiths and those of no faith at all. It is a challenge; and so is being a chaplain in today's prison service. Like Isaiah, you are to speak again and again a word which will be heard but may never be understood. You are to be prophets, yes, but priest and pastors too. Being a priest is the best job in the world. My hope and my prayer for each one of you is that you will bring humanity and divinity to those in your care, helping each of them to pursue their own spirituality.

Prayer

We pray for all who work in the prison service, especially those responsible for long term prisoners and those in solitary confinement. We pray for all prison chaplains, for their ministry of pastoral care, prophecy and worship. Be with all prisoners and their families, we pray, and give confidence to those moving out of prison and into the community, Amen.

The Gifts of the Hebrew Scriptures

It is not often that I use the Old Testament for my sermons. In fact, the last time, surprisingly enough, was my own daughter's wedding when I found myself turning to the Book of Genesis and that beautiful love story about Jacob and Rachel. Jacob had worked for Rachel for seven years but we are told 'it seemed but a few days, because he loved her'. The significance of this particular story lay in the fact that my daughter and her husband had known each other for seven years before their marriage.

The reason for talking about the Old Testament , its theology and its vast store of anecdotes and stories today is because, quite simply, the prophets are the theme for the second Sunday in Advent and the second candle in the Advent wreath. One of the post Communion sentences from Psalm 119 reads—'How sweet are the words of the Lord to the taste, sweeter than honey to the mouth. Through his precepts we get understanding.' which is a reminder to us and to the people of the Old Testament just how important their scriptures are.

There simply is not time to talk at any length about the Old Testament and so what I want to do is just pick out three themes from the Old Testament literature which seem to me to speak to our own generation. This might surprise you that something written two and a half thousand years ago and more and which really constitutes the history book of the Jewish people should have relevance for today. However, if it is part of the word of God (and we believe it is), then surely it will have an eternal quality and speak to successive generations.

The first five books of the Old Testament make up what is called the Law and here in great detail are all the laws which governed the life of the Jewish people the

Israelites. God himself was seen as a God of justice who would exact punishment when his laws were broken and be merciful both to those who had been obedient and, furthermore, in literature like the Book of Hosea, to those who had been disobedient and strayed from the truth.

It seems to me that in contemporary society we, too, shall hear more about law much of it emanating from Europe! The more talk there is about law, the more the Church needs to speak about justice to ensure that people are dealt with in a fair and just manner without prejudice and bigotry and only after all the available evidence has been gathered and heard. All this is because individuals are precious in the sight of God, so much so that he knows the number of hairs on their heads and, therefore, any abuse or affront of a person is an affront to God himself. This, of course, becomes clearer when we think of the truth and meaning of Christmas—the fact that God lived amongst us—but that is the New Testament and I need to stay with the Old Testament!

Secondly, in the New Testament the people of God are referred to as the 'Body of Christ'. We learn all about this in St Paul's writings and the emphasis is on an efficient organization in which all the different parts work together for the benefit of the whole. You will have heard many sermons about the Church as the Body of Christ and how each individual member has a part to play in the whole enterprise. However, in the Old Testament we are given a very different picture and the talk is of the people of God. They are a pilgrimage people who are led out of Egypt through the wilderness and into the Promised Land and their pilgrimage to the heart of God continues throughout their history. Perhaps, just perhaps, this is a more apt metaphor for the Church today and I say this because I am aware of the strains and stresses placed upon the institutional Church and also the disillusionment and criticisms that go along with it. Sometimes the poor old Church of England seems to be creaking at the joints and needs the ecclesiastical equivalent of an artificial hip. We live with the House Church, New Age Religion and Fellowship Churches springing up all over the place. None of these are part of the institutional Church but I think they are to be numbered among the people of God. It is for this reason that I am suggesting that the Old Testament picture of the pilgrimage people of God might be more meaningful for us today than the efficient organization called the Body of Christ. Though, having said all this, we really do need both images because both have important things to offer.

The third point is very general and really comes from reading the whole of the Old Testament as though it were one book. Let me digress for a moment. In this country it is still the case that when we meet people the conversation often begins with a comment about the weather. Talking about the weather is a conversation starter and we really are very good at it. In this sense we would have a lot in common with the Hebrew people—the Jews of the Old Testament because they, too, were very conscious of changes in the weather, in the climate and in the temperature. They were very aware of the day-to-day change from darkness to light and the ending of the day as night began. They were conscious of all of this because they had a very real belief in the presence of God in all that they did. Their God truly walked through history with them, every little thing that happened to them as individuals and to them as a nation and to them as the pilgrimage people of God was about God being present in every aspect of their lives. Their God was not relegated to the heavens, believing that God is in his heaven and all is well with the world. Their God was not some distant, unapproachable figure but someone who walked by their side. As well as being the grand Creator, he was a God who had a care and a love for all that he had created and especially for his chosen people—the Jews. Theirs, then, was a vibrant and living faith in a God who was close and accessible. It is just this sort of God that we need to rediscover in the Church today. We, too, need a God who is near, not far away, who is part of our daily lives, not divorced from reality, and who cares for all that has been created, for all that lives.

So, then, pick up your bibles and turn to the Old Testament and ponder the need for justice, the model for the Church today of the pilgrimage people of God and for a God who is involved in our day-to-day activity. Try to make sure that you have a version of the bible which includes the Apochrypha and there you will find amusing stories like Bel and the Dragon and Susannah and the Elders. Perhaps you will read stories you have never heard before and learn more about the Old Testament and the picture of God it offers to us today.

Prayer

May the law always, we pray, be tempered by justice and loving kindness and may we ever relish the storehouse of wisdom and insight offered to us in the books of the Old Testament. Lord be with us in every step we take, beside us to accompany us, behind us to support us and ahead of us to guide and direct us, Amen.

Towards Heaven and Hell

(St Matthew 11 vs. 42)
It is all rather grim—the depictions of hell in the N.T.

One of my passions is Romanesque art and architecture and, over the years, I have managed to build up quite a library of slides and powerpoints which I use for talks and seminars. Europe abounds with Romanesque churches and one of their great glories is the west front of these church buildings which were erected between 1000 and 1200 AD and which are elaborately decorated, carefully crafted and full of sculpture—sculpture which is often carved in fine and intricate detail. In the medieval mind these glorious west fronts did not only provide access into the rest of the church but were also seen as the gateway to Heaven itself. One of the major themes in the sculpture which you find displayed on the front of these wonderful churches is the Last Judgement where the division is made between those who go to Heaven and those who go to Hell. Understandably then you will find monsters and devils stationed at the gateway to Hell, devouring the damned souls whose fate has been decided. What is never revealed is the basis on which the judgement is made. You cannot see from the sculpture why one group of people should be destined for Hell and another for Heaven. Who judges and how, is to be found in the pages of the New Testament, rather than in medieval sculpture. The judgement is to be found in parables like today's Gospel, which tells us about the man who sowed his seed and the enemy who planted weeds among the good seed.

In other parables, Jesus talks about the great distinctions and divisions between the rich and the poor. The disinterested rich and the needy poor have been with us throughout the whole of history. In our own day it is often said that as the rich become richer, so the poor become poorer. Today poverty appears in myriad forms across the world. There are the starving in the Third World, refugees fleeing oppressive regimes and in our own society a whole range of people who are poor and needy.

It is nearly fourteen years since the Public Enquiry into the tragic events surrounding the death of Victoria Climbe, later known as the Leeming report because it was chaired by Lord Leeming. The events surrounding Victoria's death were well documented and her great aunt and her boyfriend were sent to prison. This is perhaps one of the worst and most unspeakable acts of child abuse ever recorded in this country and to most rational people was an act of sheer wickedness. This was wickedness meted out on an individual, a child.

The rich of this world are still alive and well and so too are the poor. It was Wilson Carlile, the Founder of the Church Army, who resigned his curacy in 1882 because of the lack of contact between the Church and the working classes. It was of real concern to him and, after leaving his curacy, he began outdoor preaching. There are many today who would say that the gap still exists and in some places has grown in size. You cannot read the Christian Gospel without coming to the conclusion that Jesus befriended the poor, sat with the poor and spent a great deal of his short ministry with the rejected, dejected and neglected. Today we ignore the poor at our peril. People like Wilson Carlile, Lord Shaftesbury and many, many others have reminded us of this truth. How are we to do this in an age which does not have the mindset of medieval society which lived in fear of the very real possibility of eternal damnation? Secular people have largely given up these beliefs and ideas, though many (and I automatically include all Christians) do not see death as the end of the pilgrimage. Ian Bradley writing in a book "Colonies of Heaven" says "We also desperately need prayers for the dying which pick up the pilgrimage theme and prepare souls for their journey out of this world and into the next. Such prayers are as important in both pastoral and spiritual terms for the living as for the dying". Another writer (Penelope Willcock) offers us these lovely words "To accompany other people, along with their loved ones, up to the gate of death is to enter Holy Ground. To stand in an awesome place where the wind of the spirit blows; to encounter peace and grief, insight, intimacy and pain on a level not found in ordinary living. By the side of the dying we learn stillness, waiting, simply being; the art of quietness and keeping watch, prayer beyond words".

There is always the hope of eternity for which careful preparation needs to be made, though it may not be portrayed in the stark and gruesome characters of medieval society. However, it is there as a possibility for all; and the wicked and disinterested rich would do well to remember this. More importantly for us, as Christians living in the 21st century, we do well to recognise and point to a truth which Jesus made clear in the parable of Dives and Lazarus. Jesus puts words into the mouth of Abraham, the Father of all Faith, who says "If they do not listen to Moses and the Prophets, neither will they be convinced even if someone rises from the dead". This surely is how the Christian Church convinces the world of the justice of God as well as the love of God. This is how Christian people draw attention to the fate of today's Dives' and today's Lazarus'. Quite simply the Church preaches the risen Christ and goes on preaching this Gospel of resurrection and reconciliation in the knowledge that human nature has not changed that much and they have not listened to Moses and the Prophets nor are they convinced even though someone *has* risen from the dead.

We know how difficult it is for people to hear unpalatable truths. We know how difficult it is for people to hear about changes that are necessary in the Church today if this Gospel of resurrection and reconciliation is to be preached from the resources available to us. We know that those resources are fairly meagre even though the world at large sees the Church of England as a rich landlord. Helping people to hear these messages is never easy and it is never easy because accepting change means changing yourself and this is something none of us really likes to do.

Preaching the Gospel begins with repentance. It was John the Baptist who encouraged the people around him to repent and be baptised. The very word for repentance means changing one's mind and so this idea of change is there from the very beginning and then continues on and on so that, in the words of the hymn, "We are changed from glory to glory so that we too can take our place with the angels around the throne of God".

Prayer

As we journey through this life, help us, we pray, to make right choices and arrive at the gates of heaven. May we devote our ministries to those whom Jesus befriended and supported, so that we too may espouse those values which bring us nearer to your heavenly throne, Amen.

Who is this Jesus?

'Withal praying also for us, that God would open unto us a door of utterance, *to speak the mystery of Christ*, for which I am also in bonds' (Col.4 v.3)

I was in Cardiff in order to spend a morning giving lectures to the new mental health chaplains about mental health law, theology and spirituality. Earlier at the Eucharist we celebrated the birth of the Blessed Virgin Mary and somehow I had to link this with mental health.

I found myself asking questions about how Mary coped with her bereavement after Jesus' death and was Jesus depressed in the garden of Gethsemane and did he ever experience psychosis. The questions about Jesus were christological, that is to say they raised questions about who Jesus was and how we understand the man Jesus and the Christ of faith.

In the gospels it was Jesus' identity that had always been uppermost in the minds of the Jewish authorities who were keen to learn who this Jesus was. In today's epistle St Paul's reference to 'the mystery of Christ' is a christological question.

That he was born in a stable, died on a cross where the townsfolk of Jerusalem tipped their rubbish and was buried in a borrowed grave suggests that he was either going to sink without trace or turn heads. As you know he turned heads and in 'One Solitary Life' we read:

Here is a man who was born in an obscure village, the child of a peasant woman. He grew up in another village. He worked in a carpenter's shop until He was thirty. Then for three years He was an itinerant preacher.

He never owned a home. He never wrote a book. He never held an office. He never had a family. He never went to college.

He never put His foot inside a big city. He never travelled more than two hundred miles from the place where He was born. He never did one of the things that usually accompany greatness. He had no credentials but Himself...

While still a young man, the tide of popular opinion turned against him. His friends ran away. One of them denied Him. He was turned over to His enemies. He went through the mockery of a trial. He was nailed upon a cross between two thieves. While He was dying His executioners gambled for the only piece of property He had on earth—His coat. When He was dead, He was laid in a borrowed grave through the pity of a friend.

Nineteen long centuries have come and gone, and today He is a centre piece of the human race. I am well within the mark when I say that all the armies that ever marched, all the navies that were ever built; all the parliaments that ever sat and all the kings that ever reigned, put together, have not affected the life of man upon this earth as powerfully as has that one solitary life.

(This was adapted from a sermon by Dr James Allan Francis in "The Real Jesus and Other Sermons" © 1926)

The question—the christological question—of who Jesus is has been asked in every generation since. It was actually asked by Jesus himself on the mount of the Transfiguration—Who do people say that I am. Throughout the gospel, it is the most unlikely people who respond to Jesus, who believe in him and who identify who he is, from blind Bartimaeus to tax gatherers.

Identity, however, is only one element of christology. There is so much more to unpack and the core of the question is reconciling Jesus as both man and God. We must start with the man Jesus and try to spell out the meaning of Christ from below as it were, where we ourselves are. We cannot really start with the Trinitarian God above and move to the man Jesus below because that would presuppose that we can enter the mind of God. So we start where we are and this accords with the great cry from Irenaeus that God became man so that we could become divine.

There are two tasks viz: to express and explain the presence of the full divinity of God in the man Jesus showing how he is both truly God and truly man, and to bring out the difference between God and man in Jesus—avoiding the sort of confusion where Jesus would be neither fully divine nor fully human.

There have been, as you may imagine, innumerable theories put forward and one whole creed, the Athanasian, is devoted to Jesus' identity. Since 1800, tens of thousands of books on christology have appeared. At the Council of Chalcedon in 451, it was said that Jesus has two natures in one person. Moving quickly through history to Martin Luther who asked ' How can I find a gracious God?' and, like other reformers who followed him, concentrated on the nature of the gift of divine presence; but sadly that does not move us any further forward.

Modern theologians have tended to stress one or other of the two natures of Jesus and in Latin America it is Jesus' commitment to the poor and dispossessed which predominates—the people who, we have already noted, readily identify Jesus. One question often asked is when Jesus suffered on the cross, did God? If not, why not!

My own approach is to encourage a belief not in a dead Jesus but in a living Christ, though there are many folk today who acknowledge Jesus as a good man, wonderful teacher, compassionate healer, and reformer but cannot name him as Son of God. I believe that in his person Jesus reveals both the glory of God and the glory of man equally. You will have your own views on the identity of Jesus and some of you may remember Bishop John Robinson of 'Honest to God' fame. Let me end with what he said—that Jesus is a window and through the window we see God, Amen.

Prayer

Almighty God whose son, Jesus Christ, lived the life we live, plumbed the depths of human experience and gave his life that we may live in harmony with you and one another. Help us to celebrate Jesus the man and the Christ of faith and, we pray, enter into divine glory, Amen.

Marriage

John's Gospel has always occupied a special place for me because its style, construction and theology is very different from the other three gospels, which is well illustrated by John's reliance upon signs to express truths about God and Jesus. He also writes in such a way that there are layers to the text and every time you read a passage, you spot something new; it is as though there are meanings within meanings within meanings.

In the Gospel itself one of my favourite passages is the wedding at Cana in Galilee. It has much to tell us about family life, though in the popular mind is remembered more particularly for the amount of wine that was consumed at the wedding feast. Those six stone pots that Jesus blessed would have held about thirty gallons each. Even for a reasonably sized guest list that was still an enormous quantity of wine.

The miracle of the wedding at Cana is one of the first signs and the opening sentence sets the context. We read that it took place on the third day. I do not believe that this was a coincidence but something that John wants us to note carefully. The context for the wedding is that of the third day and it is on the third day that Jesus rose again. We understand from this that weddings are to be associated with new life and new beginnings. We could do worse than rely upon the symbols and expressions of Easter to help us understand marriage and family life. Easter continues to be a favourite time of the year for weddings and I hope that people have made the link between marriage and Easter.

From the egg-shaped tomb rises the promise of moving ever deeper into the mystery of God and the mystery of each other. This is what I call the Heineken factor. It is that aspect of marriage which is paradoxically both private and public. It offers the possibility of going where we have never been before, to parts still unexplored and to the very heart of our own mystery.

Marriage, like Easter, reaches those parts of our experience, the depth of our being and the outer most fringes of our faith which have not been reached before. Easter resurrection is a celebration of the other side of ourselves. This is the side that God sees and this is the side which is the gateway to eternity. Here we can step into the very presence of God himself where we celebrate a beginning, not an end. This is really a journey of exploration coupled with the insight that, what we so often see as an end, is really a beginning. T.S. Eliot sums it up well in one of his poems:

We shall not cease from exploration,
and the end of all our exploring
will be to arrive where we started
and know the place for the first time.

What we call the beginning is often the end
and to make an end is to make a beginning.
The end is where we start from.

Secondly we note the miracle is the change of water into wine. Anyone who makes their own wine knows that this is a continuous process and that subtle changes take place during fermentation. Here is a metaphor for marriage itself. Two people set out on the most intimate relationship known to human beings and a process of change is begun. There are likely to be all sorts of moments in the marriage relationship—happy, fiery, sad, joyful, creative—the list is a very long one. What troubles me are those people who, often after years of marriage, say we never had a cross word and I think to myself how little change must have taken place in that relationship. Change is the means by which human relationships develop and grow. It is part of the vocation of marriage that we are called to be agents of change for each other.

At the end of the Gospel reading, we are told that this was the first sign by which Jesus revealed his glory. St John uses seven signs altogether throughout the Gospel to direct our attention to the activity of God in human affairs and how we are to understand that activity. The marriage at Cana is the first sign and this means that God's glory is revealed first in a marriage, in a family, in the closest knit human group that has developed throughout history. God's glory is not to be seen first in a great cathedral or abbey church, nor from the summit of a mountain, nor in a beautiful garden, nor in a haunting melody, but first and foremost in the loving relationship we call marriage.

Do these insights relate to today and the society in which live? The quick answer is that the truths of the wedding at Cana in Galilee are needed more today than ever before. We know that stimulating and supporting family life in our own society is vital because family life is becoming more and more fragile and communities are breaking down. More than any other factor, it is probably individualism which pervades our society and erodes family and community life. Individualism is not the same as valuing and supporting individuals in families and communities. Individualism is about each person being their own world. Rather than 'no man being an island ....', it is more accurate to say that everyone is an island! Moral values, ethical codes, spirituality, expectations of relationships—all of these are determined by each person for themselves. Everything becomes relative to what we want, rather than what we need. The accelerated move towards individualism is underlined by statistics like 40% of all households in the country being occupied by one person. If we are to recapture the richness of family life and the growth and development of human relationships which is promoted by good social interaction, then the miracle at Cana needs to be taken seriously. It spells out unequivocally that marriage and family life is where wholesome, creative and new relationships can best be nurtured. It encourages us to meet the challenge of change head on and it reminds us that the glory of God is to be found in loving faithful relationships between one person and another. We can only ever start with ourselves; but here is something to challenge us, to celebrate and share with others as each of us in our own way seeks to capture the glory of God, Amen.

Hearing Others' Voices

Hearing Others' Voices: A transcultural and transdisciplinary book series in simple and straightforward language, to inform and engage general readers, undergraduates and, above all, sixth formers in recent advances in thought, unaccountably overlooked areas of the world, and key issues of the day.

CPSIA information can be obtained
at www.ICGtesting.com
Printed in the USA
BVHW030216030619
549975BV00001B/57/P

9 781911 221654